Reading
Social Studies

Dr. Kylene Beers

HOLT, RINEHART AND WINSTON

A Harcourt Education Company

Orlando • **Austin** • New York • San Diego • London

Kylene Beers, Ed.D.
Senior Reading Researcher
Comer School Development Program
Yale University
New Haven, Connecticut

Kylene Beers, the Vice President–Elect of the National Council of Teachers of English, is a Senior Reading Researcher in the Comer School Development Program of the Child Study Center at Yale University. A former middle school teacher, Kylene has turned her commitment to helping struggling readers into the major focus of her research, writing, speaking, and teaching. She is a program author for *Holt Literature and Language Arts,* grades 6–12, and *Elements of Literature,* grades 6–12; author of *When Kids Can't Read/What Teachers Can Do* (Heinemann, 2002) and the forthcoming book *Thinking Through Reading: Comprehension, Fluency, and Vocabulary Strategies for Struggling Readers* (Heinemann, 2006); co-editor of *Into Focus: Understanding and Creating Middle School Readers* (Christopher-Gordon, 1998); and co-editor of *Books for You: An Annotated Booklist for High School Students* (NCTE, 2000). A respected authority on struggling readers who works with elementary, middle school, and high school teachers across the nation, Kylene was the 2001 recipient of the Richard W. Halle Award given by NCTE for outstanding contributions to middle school education.

ISBN 0-03-079776-4

6 7 8 9 018 09 08

Contents

To the Teacher iv
To the Student v
Learning and Thinking and Reading: Discovering that Connection in the
   Social Studies Classroom, by Dr. Kylene Beers 1
The Reading Process 8

Reading Skills
Setting a Purpose 9
Making Predictions 14
Identifying Main Ideas and Details 19
Summarizing 24
Making Inferences 29
Sequencing 34
Identifying Cause and Effect 39
Comparing and Contrasting 44
Identifying Problems and Solutions 49
Drawing Conclusions 54
Making Generalizations 59

Think-Alouds
How to Use Think-Alouds with Your Students 64
Types of Think-Aloud Comments 66
Think-Alouds: Reading American History 67
Think-Alouds: Reading World History 71
Think-Alouds: Reading Geography 75
Think-Alouds: Reading Civics 79

Graphic Organizers
How to Use Graphic Organizers 83
Graphic Organizers 85

Answer Key 97

All reading selections in *Reading Social Studies* are taken from passages in the *Holt Social Studies* textbooks listed below.

Pages	*Holt Social Studies* Title / © year
9, 29, 30, 34, 55, 59, 60, 67, 68	*United States History* 2007
10, 15, 20, 25, 35, 40, 45, 50, 69, 70	*American Anthem* 2007
11, 16, 21, 24, 26, 31, 36, 39, 41, 46, 51, 54, 56, 61, 71, 72, 73, 74	*World History* 2006
12, 49	*Africa* 2007
13, 18, 23, 28, 33, 38, 43, 48, 53, 58, 63, 79, 80, 81, 82	*Civics in Practice* 2007
14, 52	*Europe and Russia* 2007
17, 19, 22, 27, 32, 42, 44, 47, 77, 78	*World Geography Today* 2005
37, 76	*Introduction to Geography* 2007
57	*Southwest and Central Asia* 2007
62, 75	*The Americas* 2007

To the Teacher

Reading Social Studies provides you with different tools to help your students become better readers. The activities are usable in any social studies course and can meet the varied learning styles of students. With content designed by Dr. Kylene Beers, this book consists of the following elements:

- Reading Skills
- Think-Alouds
- Graphic Organizers

Each element is designed to provide your students with practice in breaking down the information in their textbooks to get the most meaning. In addition to providing valuable explanation and practice for your students, the activities will help you determine which students are reading with understanding and which ones need additional assistance.

Reading Skills

Each lesson teaches a different reading skill, such as finding main ideas or comparing and contrasting. For each skill, a one-page lesson with example can be used to provide step-by-step instructions for your students about how to read their textbooks effectively. Also included for each skill are practice pages, with one passage each relating to American history, world history, geography, and civics. The graphic organizers on the practice pages will help your students follow logical steps and organize their thoughts as they reach their goal of grasping the content of the passage.

Think-Alouds

Think-Alouds are designed to help your students move beyond just reading the words on the page and to really engage with their reading. The Think-Aloud strategy encourages students to pause occasionally as they read in order to think aloud about the connections they are making, images they are creating, and problems they are having with understanding. The samples provided can be used as classroom activities, in small groups, or independently. A separate introduction to Think-Alouds explains the many ways to use these activities in your classroom.

Graphic Organizers

Graphic organizers are a valuable tool for teaching social studies. Included in this book are graphic organizers that students can fill out on their own. In a separate introduction to the graphic organizers section, you will find suggestions about topics for which each graphic organizer is best suited. Each graphic organizer can be used with your choice of content, allowing you to provide reading support that is appropriate for whatever subject your students are studying at the time.

Reading Social Studies

To the Student

This book is designed to help you read your social studies books. It contains activities that will help you learn how to focus on important information and discover meaning as you read. This book has the following three parts:

- Reading Skills
- Think-Alouds
- Graphic Organizers

Each part focuses on specific skills or strategies you can use to improve your reading.

Reading Skills

Here you will find lessons that teach different reading skills, such as finding main ideas or comparing and contrasting. For each skill, read the page of explanation and follow along with the example. Then you can practice the skill on your own with the worksheets. These worksheets contain passages taken directly from your social studies book and graphic organizers to help you organize the information and your thinking as you read.

Think-Alouds

Think-Alouds are fun! When you do a Think-Aloud, you practice thinking about what you are reading. Thinking about your reading will help you make connections between the content and what you already know. Passages used in the Think-Alouds are taken directly from your social studies book. You can use the Think-Aloud examples in this book to see the kinds of comments other students have made as they have read. When you get the idea, you can use the Think-Aloud Comments Sheet to remind you to "think aloud" as you read any passage from your textbook.

Graphic Organizers

Graphic organizers are helpful for organizing information as you read. This book has several different types of large graphic organizers, so you can choose the type that works best for whatever topic you are reading about. You can use these graphic organizers to take notes and as a study tool to help you prepare for important tests.

Reading Social Studies

Learning and Thinking and Reading:
Discovering that Connection in the Social Studies Classroom

By Kylene Beers, Ed.D.

"So, Marcus, what are you supposed to be doing right now," I asked the fifteen-year-old eighth grader who was supposed to be reading a chapter in his social studies book.

The response was a shrug of the shoulders.

I tried again. "Marcus, shouldn't you be reading the chapter?"

Marcus slowly lifted hooded eyes and said, "Reading stinks."

I took that to mean that Marcus wouldn't be reading his chapter in his social studies book.

* * * *

Marcus had decided that reading wasn't a preferred activity for a specific reason: this eighth grader reads at about a third grade level. I can't fault Marcus for not wanting to do something that he can't do well. There are few things that I, as a confident, self-assured adult, rush to do when I know that I won't be successful at the endeavor. Why should Marcus, an adolescent struggling to maintain any type of self-esteem, be willing to do something day after day after day when he believes he will in all likelihood not be successful? Marcus labels reading a negative activity because the alternative—acknowledging his inability to read at grade level—is too difficult, too embarrassing, and makes him too vulnerable. Far safer for the response to be "reading stinks" than "I don't know some of the words; I can't figure out the meaning."

That afternoon, when school was over, I talked with Marcus's social studies teacher:

"Marcus is certainly having trouble," I said.

"Well, he can't read, and he won't try, and the textbook is hard for him. It's a real problem," he replied.

"What do you think you could do to help Marcus the most?" I asked.

His teacher leaned back in his desk chair, balancing it on the back two legs, and chewed on a pencil end for a long moment. He stared at me, narrowing his eyes. Finally, decisively, he brought his chair forward, put his elbows on his desk, pointed his pencil at me and answered my question: "You want to help Marcus?" He didn't wait for an answer. "You want to help that kid read this book?" he asked tapping the textbook on his desk and then continued not waiting for my reply. "Then, the reality is, you've got to show me what to do because I'm no reading teacher. I didn't sign on to be a reading teacher and I'm tired of people telling me that every teacher is a reading teacher. I'm not. I teach social studies. I thought I'd be teaching kids about cultures and governments and the development of societies and how people interact with one another and their environment. I never anticipated that eighth graders wouldn't know how to read their books. I'm not talking about they don't *want* to read them—you expect that. I'm saying I've got kids who *can't* read them. I never expected that whether I wanted to or not I'd need to teach reading."

He paused to draw a breath and then concluded: "You know, I've got a lot of kids like Marcus in each class, and quite honestly, I don't have a clue what to do with them. Not one clue. So, if you want to help Marcus, you've got to first help me." He stopped and with eyes still narrowed waited for my answer.

And so, we began.

Turning a Field of Dreams into Reality

Being an effective reading teacher requires more than the edict from the central administration office that states that "All teachers are teachers of reading." The "if we decree it, it will happen" mantra will remain but a field of dreams if specific information isn't shared with those teachers who prior to the memo didn't see themselves as reading teachers—teachers like Mike, Marcus's social studies teacher.

Mike's challenge to me was the right one. To help Mike, I had to start by making sure he understood important reading processes; then we had to move to looking at how those processes could fit into the social studies curriculum. Mike already had much to cover with his regular curriculum. Teaching reading processes in his classroom couldn't be about adding more to an already packed scope and sequence. Instead, I had to show him how reading processes could be used while teaching social studies so that students could more easily and quickly learn the social studies content. We began with Mike's first question.

"I don't know what to do when kids really just can't even read the textbook."

When I asked Mike how he knew Marcus couldn't read the book, he explained that when he asked Marcus questions about what he had read, Marcus either didn't know the answers or admitted that he hadn't read the chapter. "I just figured that meant he couldn't read it—you know, couldn't figure out the words," Mike explained. It's a natural assumption, but it may be a wrong one. Mike had confused decoding with understanding. He presumed that since Marcus couldn't show that he understood what he read that he therefore hadn't been able to decode the words. This confusion reveals a belief that decoding automatically leads to understanding. But, there are many times when that isn't true. Show me a medical textbook and while I can say the words aloud, I wouldn't be able to explain to you what I've read. (The same is often true for the instructions that are supposed to show me in seven easy steps how to program my VCR to record at particular times!) Decoding is a part of reading—but only a part.

Indeed, most of the students who struggle with reading in your middle school classroom don't struggle at the word level. They can decode—or sound out—the words. Instead, the more likely problems are problems with fluency or with comprehension. But, if you think that decoding is a problem for a particular student, then ask the student to read aloud a little bit of the text to you.

> **Keep in Mind:** Reading aloud will be embarrassing for the student if decoding is a problem, so this needs to happen one-on-one. Give the student a pass to come in during lunch. Or when others are reading or working in small groups, take this student out in the hall to read to you. You don't need much time with the student—just long enough to decide if he can't figure out how to say the words or can decode the words but is just decoding very slowly. This is a critical difference.

As the student reads to you, listen for miscues—mistakes in reading. If the student gets stuck on a word, don't immediately offer the word. Wait for several seconds to see if the student can figure it out. If not, go ahead and supply the word, but make a mental note about what happened. Later, think about the words that the student missed (miscued). Decide if the student is missing uncommon words—such as *principality, feudalism,* or *monarchy*—or more common words—such as *because, however,* and *kingdom*. If the student is missing the common words, then this student needs reading support beyond what you will be offering in your classroom. This student needs specific intervention with a focus on word recognition skills. Talk to the language arts teacher or the reading coach or literacy coach in your school to make sure that student is getting the support with word recognition that he needs.

However, if the student stumbles over words that you're fairly sure he's only encountering in his social studies book (How often do you find *Phoenicians* mentioned in the sports section of the newspaper or in a current popular magazine?) then tell the student the word, maybe point out some quick, easy decoding pointers—"remember that <u>ph</u> together makes the /f/ sound like at the beginning of phone"—and then make sure the student sees the word often over the next several days.

Reading Defined: When you see a letter or letters between diagonal slashes, don't say the letter, but instead say the sound the letter makes. So, when you see /f/ you don't say letter *f* but instead say the sound heard at the beginning of the word fish.

Next, remember that it is hard to learn a new word if you don't see if often. Here are some ways to help your students learn to recognize an uncommon word:

- Use it in a sentence as you write the sentence on the overhead projector ("Today, we'll continue talking about the Phoenicians.").

- Put it on a bulletin board and read aloud what's on the bulletin board ("Life and Accomplishments of the Phoenicians").

- Print the word on a large card that you hold up as students enter the classroom giving them extra points if they can tell you the word and define it.

The point is to give them multiple opportunities to see the written word and hear it in oral contexts.

Once you've listened to a student read, you might discover that even though he's calling all the words, he's reading very slowly (or sometimes is reading very, very fast). This student has a problem with fluency.

Reading Defined: Reading fluency is about three things: the ability to decode words quickly (automaticity), the ability to decode with accuracy, and the ability to read with the proper expression (so noting punctuation).

Students with fluency problems might do one or several of the following:

- Read very slowly, a word at a time

- Ignore punctuation, including commas, periods, question marks, semi-colons, hyphens, and parenthesis

- Use little or no expression when reading

- Occasionally read too fast—again with no expression and no consideration of punctuation

- Decode words incorrectly and not correct the mistake

- Decode words incorrectly and note the mistake and go back to self-correct

Again, if what you note as the student reads is that the student consistently miscues on common words and does not self-correct these mistakes, then this student needs specialized intervention. However, if the problem is with rate of reading, you can help. You might try these two methods.

1. Help students develop a "reader's ear." Students who read too slowly often haven't developed what Eudora Welty labeled a "reader's ear." This means they don't have that internal voice telling them what reading should sound like. To develop a reader's ear, students need to hear a skilled reader reading aloud. Disfluent readers benefit the most when they can hear you read as they follow along in their textbooks. Suddenly they hear the emphasis your voice gives to bold-faced words; they hear you pause when you come to commas or end punctuation; they hear the way your voice sort of hangs, anticipating what's next, when you encounter a colon.

Keep in Mind: Disfluent readers must learn that punctuation is a signpost to meaning—and that can't happen if you aren't spending at least a few minutes each day reading a portion of the text to them. You might even put a paragraph (short one!) on a transparency and show it on the overhead projector as you read it aloud. Then go back and read it again asking students to tell you what certain punctuation tells them to do.

---

2. Look at the chapters in your textbook. Find some of the short introductions to chapters or the summaries at ends of sections or the biography sections. Put students into pairs and have one person from each pair read aloud that short section to the partner. Let the partner use the second hand on the classroom clock or perhaps on a watch to time how long it takes the reader to get through the section. Then have the reader read that section a second and third time. Let the partner time the reader each time. Remind the reader that the point isn't to rush, but to read at a rate that is comfortable and expressive. Chances are the third reading will be faster than the first. Do this every day for several weeks. Students can stay with the same passage for two or three days and then turn to another passage. Two things will happen. First, they will really learn the material in that passage! Second, eventually, the first timed reading starts at about the same rate as the original third timed reading. In other words, the fluency practice from one passage transfers to the next passage. Why? For the same reason that practicing one piano piece helps you learn to read another piano piece or practicing golf on one course helps you play on another course or learning about one society helps you learn more easily about another society.

You Decide: Fluency or Word Recognition Problem?

The following represents the way Marcus read a few of the lines from a social studies text. The dots (…) between words indicate the pauses he took between words. The more dots you see, the longer the pause he took. You won't see any capitalized words because he disregarded all end punctuation. As you read this transcript, ask yourself whether Marcus has a problem with word recognition or with fluency.

Marcus: "Most…S-Su-mer-ian Sumerian…most Summary Sumerian…rulers…lived…in.large… p-palaces…other…rich…Sum-Sumerians…had…had..two…store…two-story…homes…with a… as…as…many…as…a…do-doz-en…rooms…most…people…how…most…people…how-ever… however…lived…in…smaller…one…one…story…houses…these houses…homes…had…six… or…sev-en…rooms………a-ar…arranged…around…a…small….a small…co-courthouse…. courtyard." (p. 68 *World History*)

If you decided that Marcus had a problem with fluency, you're correct. He's actually got good decoding skills; what he lacks is automaticity. That means that he can't quickly decode the words so his reading sounds like what you'd hear from a beginning reader.

So, if he can decode most of the words, and his reading sounds smooth, then what's his problem?

When word recognition and fluency aren't the problems, then the problem might lie with comprehension—that important ability to understand what's read. Students who come from elementary programs that overemphasize phonics have often had little instruction into *how* to comprehend a text. And sometimes teachers—who are good readers—have so internalized the comprehension processes that they can't really explain what they do as they read. But if you'll go read a text that is difficult for you (ask a language arts teacher to bring in a college poetry book or have the science teacher loan you an advanced chemistry text) and take some notes on what you're doing as you're reading it to make it make sense, you'll probably discover that you've done the following types of things:

- Visualized something happening in the text
- Noted the parts that are confusing
- Predicted where the text is going next
- Clarified confusing parts by rereading, deciding to read on, looking up unknown vocabulary, refering to charts, maps, footnotes, or asking someone for help
- Summarized sections as you read
- Connected what you were reading to what you already knew

Each of those things you do in order to make the text make sense are comprehension processes. You do these things so automatically that you probably aren't even aware of them. For instance, when you don't understand something, you're brain might note what was confusing without you consciously saying to yourself, "Now I'm confused at this part." Instead, it's almost like you just sense it, that "huh?" feeling is there and you quickly decide whether your attention had wandered and whether you need to reread or if reading on is the best solution.

However, many of the struggling readers who sit in your classroom have never internalized these processes. Consequently, you need to show them how you use these processes with the content in their textbook so that they can do the same thing. The best way to do this is with a strategy called think-aloud.

Reading Defined: Don't get confused. A comprehension process is the thinking we do as we figure something out. Like all thinking, it's invisible. To pull that invisible process out to the visible level, we use strategies. Think-aloud is a strategy that shows students the processes you use when figuring out a text. This guidebook will show you several additional strategies.

To model a think-aloud, you simply read aloud a short text (one or two paragraphs is more than enough) pausing to tell students how you've figured out something. I like to put the paragraph on a transparency to show it on the overhead projector, but you can also have students just turn to the paragraph in their book and follow along. I like to use the transparency so I can underline things or make notes in the margin as I model the think aloud for the students. To be most effective—in other words to turn this into something that students do as they read—you have to model this often. Often means several times a week for most of the year. But, this activity takes only about 5 minutes and it's explaining content that the students need. This is a perfect example of how you are teaching comprehension and simultaneously teaching your content.

Here's an example of a think-aloud I modeled for Marcus.

"Marcus—why don't you follow along here in your book as I read this paragraph aloud? You're going to hear me stop several times to think aloud about parts I've been reading. In particular, you're going to hear me talk about visualizing, identifying confusing parts, figuring out what to do when I'm confused, and making connections. Those are all things skilled readers do when they read." Note—next I read a paragraph aloud to Marcus, interrupting myself at points where I had decided I wanted to show him how I did those things just listed. I've shown this interaction between the text and my thinking in the chart below.

What the text said

The Greeks lived on rocky, mountainous lands surrounded by water.

The mainland of Greece is a peninsula, an area of land that is surrounded on three sides by water. But the Greek peninsula is very irregular. It's one big peninsula made up of a series of smaller peninsulas.

The land and sea intertwine like your hand and fingers in a bowl of water.

What I said

I can visualize this easily. The land has lots of mountains that are rocky and all around is water. Visualizing the text helps me keep up with what's happening.

At first, when it said Greece was a peninsula I wondered if I was going to remember what that was, but I decided to just keep on reading and saw that the word was defined for me. Figuring out what's confusing and deciding what to do is something skilled readers do when they read. I also wasn't very sure what the book meant by saying it was irregular. I think a regular peninsula would be like one you see more often, so an irregular one would have to be one that makes it different. By reading on to the next sentence I found out why Greece is considered to be an irregular peninsula.

I can really visualize this easily. I can see my hand in a bowl of water and see how the water is all around my fingers. As I read about this peninsula, I'm reminded of another peninsula we just read about—Italy. However, Italy wasn't made up of a series of smaller peninsulas. Making this connection to Italy so I can think about how the two are alike and different is something else skilled readers do when they read.

Once I finished with that final comment I then looked at Marcus and summarized for him what I had just done. "So, Marcus, you can see that reading is about thinking—and sometimes that thinking is about visualizing; other times it's about figuring out what's confusing; and other times it's about trying to make connections. Now, I want you to read the next couple of paragraphs and try doing the same type of thinking."

Keep in Mind: When you model a think-aloud, choose two or three comprehension processes and focus on those. Before you begin the think-aloud, tell students what processes you'll be focusing on. As you stop and explain your thinking, label the process as you use it. After you finish the passage, do two things. First, remind the students that you did those things because that's the type of thinking skilled readers do as they read. Second, remind students to try the same types of thinking as they read. If you focus on the following comprehension processes as you model think-alouds, your students will not only learn a lot about how to think through a text, but they will also learn a lot about the content you are using as your model: Predicting, Visualizing, Noting confusions, Clarifying strategies, Connecting, Asking questions, and Summarizing.

"How do I help students keep these thinking processes in their minds as they read?"

For students to internalize comprehension processes, you've got to model them often (three or four times a week) all year long. Remember, you aren't modeling the processes in isolation. You're using the processes to show students how to figure out content you want them to read. Modeling isn't enough, though. Use chart paper to make a big poster in your classroom titled "Thinking Through the Text," and make a bulleted list of the comprehension processes. Remind students of these processes often. Also, you might reproduce the worksheet found on the next page for students to use as a before, during, and after reading guide. This type of guide will help struggling readers stay focused on what they need to be doing as they read through the text.

So, "If I teach these processes, will they read?"

As a social studies teacher, you probably have a limited amount of time to help with word recognition problems. So remember, if students struggle with common words, be sure to enlist the help of the reading specialist in your school; but if the problem is fluency or comprehension, you help them with those things through the social studies content. You'll be helping them become more skilled readers—which in turn should encourage them to read. However, remember, that much of reading is about desire. You're the social studies expert—so you're the best one to know how to introduce that chapter on the Roman Empire or the Maya civilization in ways that makes students want to read to discover more! Motivation to read comes from your excitement, your ability to connect the past to the present, and your desire to make learning interesting. Consequently, to answer the question, if you help them with fluency and comprehension processes, they *will* read better. But if you ignore the critical component of motivation, then they may choose not to read—even if they have the ability.

And what about Marcus?

Mike slowly began using the think-aloud strategy along with many of the graphic organizers presented in this book with Marcus over several months. When I next saw Marcus, he was reading his social studies book in class one day. After class I asked him how the reading was going. His comments left me smiling:

"You know, Mr. Williams, he started doing this think-aloud thing with us every day. Just for a paragraph or so. I never knew how much *thinking* goes into reading. I mean why do they even bother to call it reading? And then he was like we had to do it too. He had me come in at lunch some to do it aloud with him, but now I just do it in my head while I read. Well, at first, it made my head hurt it was so much. I mean with like almost every word you could be thinking. [pause] But I noticed that when you do all the thinking with it, then you like learn a lot more. It's like learning and thinking and reading, they are like all connected in some way. That's like really important to understand."

Yes it is, Marcus. Yes, indeed.

Kylene Beers

The Reading Process

Getting Ready to Read	As I Read	After I Read
Pilots go through a checklist before they begin flying. You too should use a checklist to make sure you are ready to read.	Use the following questions to help clarify meaning as you read.	Use this space to reflect on what you've read.

Getting Ready to Read

Pilots go through a checklist before they begin flying. You too should use a checklist to make sure you are ready to read.

Titles
1. What's the title?
2. What predictions about content can I make from the title?
3. What predictions can I make from the subheadings?

Vocabulary
4. Is there a list of vocabulary words or key terms that I need to look over before I begin to read?
5. Did I divide the vocabulary words into words I know, words I've heard, words I don't know at all?

Special Features
6. What do the maps, charts, illustrations, or timelines tell me?
7. Did I review the information found in the section openers?
8. Can I state my purpose for reading this section? What am I supposed to be learning?

_____

Vocabulary to Learn

As I Read

Use the following questions to help clarify meaning as you read.

Visualizing: Can I picture this in my mind? What words help me create that picture?

Connecting: How is this (detail) like some other (detail)? How is this (person/character) like another?

Questioning: What part has confused me? What names or terms do I need to review? Can I put events in the right time order?

Clarifying: Should I reread? Read on? Can I point to where I'm confused? Can I explain what is confusing me? Should I look again at graphics? Would looking up a word in a dictionary help? Should I ask for some help?

Seeing Relationships: Do I understand the causes or effects of this event?

Predicting: Based on what I've read, what do I think will happen next? Are there signal words like *however, additionally,* or *in conclusion* that give me an idea of what's next?

Summarizing: Can I discuss what I've just read in my own words?

_____

I am confused about …

After I Read

Use this space to reflect on what you've read.

The main idea of this part was…

The summary of this section is…

Three questions I'd like to ask are

1.

2.

3.

A part where I'm still confused is…

Important dates or ideas from this section are…

Vocabulary, key terms, or names I need to review…

When you go on a trip, you have a purpose or a destination in mind before you start. Sometimes you need a map to get to your destination. When you read, you should also have a purpose in mind. This purpose keeps you focused and moving toward your goal of understanding.

As you read your textbook, you may feel lost or like you are going to a completely new place. However, textbooks provide "maps," or clues, to help you figure out where you are going. These clues are text features, such as a chapter's title, headings, pictures, and study tips. Text features can help you set a purpose for your reading.

HOW TO SET A PURPOSE

To set a purpose, follow these three basic steps:

1. **Look over the text features in the section you are about to read.** Notice headings, outlines, margin notes, and pictures.

2. **Ask yourself questions based on the text features.** Find something that interests you and then ask yourself a question about the topic.

3. **Set a purpose to guide your reading and answer your questions.** Your purpose might start out like this: "I'll read to find out about…"

President Adams and the XYZ Affair

When the diplomats arrived in France, they learned that French foreign minister Talleyrand would not speak with them. Instead, they had a strange and secret visit from three French agents. Shockingly, the agents said that Talleyrand would discuss a treaty only in exchange for a $250,000 bribe. The French government also wanted a loan of $12 million. The amazed diplomats refused these demands.

In March 1798 President Adams told Congress that the peace-seeking mission had failed. He described the French terms, substituting the letters X, Y, and Z for the names of the French agents. Upon hearing the disgraceful news, Federalists in Congress called for war with France.

The XYZ affair, as the French demand for a bribe came to be called, outraged the American public.

1. Notice text features such as headings, pictures, or tips.
This heading mentions President Adams and some affair involving letters.

2. Ask questions about the text features.
I wonder what the XYZ affair is. How did it get such a strange name? What was its impact?

3. Set a purpose for your reading.
I'll read to find out more about the XYZ affair.

From *United States History*, Launching the Nation

Setting a Purpose

As you read about American history you will come across a lot of new information. Setting a purpose can help keep you focused and moving toward your goal of understanding.

YOU TRY IT!

Use text features to help you set a purpose that will guide your reading. Complete the graphic organizer to help you through the steps of setting a purpose.

Devastation in the Dust Bowl

In the midst of the economic disaster, nature delivered a cruel blow. Around 1931 much of the Great Plains region entered a long, severe dry spell. This drought, or period of below-average rainfall, lasted for several years. By the time it lifted, millions of people had fled the area.

The great dust storms Drought is a part of a weather cycle, naturally occurring on the Great Plains every few decades. By the 1930s, however, careless agricultural practices had left the region vulnerable. Land once covered with grasses now lay bare to the sky with no vegetation to hold the soil in place.

When the storms came, they stripped away the topsoil and blew it hundreds of miles away. In some of the worst storms, dust reached as far as the Atlantic Coast. Drifting mounds of dust choked crops and buried farm equipment. The fine dust blew into homes through drafty windows and under doors. Year after year, storms came and wreaked destruction. The hardest hit area— including parts of Oklahoma, Kansas, Colorado, New Mexico, and Texas—became known as the Dust Bowl.

From *American Anthem*, The Great Depression Begins

Pick a heading that interests you.

_____
_____
_____
_____
_____
_____

▼

Ask yourself a question about the heading.

_____
_____
_____
_____
_____
_____

▼

Set a purpose for your reading.

_____
_____
_____
_____
_____
_____
_____

Setting a Purpose

Reading Skills

Reading World History

As you read about world history you will come across a lot of new information. Setting a purpose can help keep you focused and moving toward your goal of understanding.

YOU TRY IT!

Use text features to help you set a purpose that will guide your reading. Complete the graphic organizer to help you through the steps of setting a purpose.

Section 3: Greek Mythology and Literature

What You Will Learn…
Main Ideas

1. The Greeks created myths to explain the world.
2. Ancient Greek literature provides some of the world's greatest poems and stories.
3. Greek literature lives in and influences our world even today.

The Big Idea

The ancient Greeks created great myths and works of literature that influence the way we speak and write today.

Key Terms and People

mythology
Homer
Sappho
Aesop
fables

Building Background

The Greeks lived in a time long before the development of science. To them, natural events like thunderstorms and changing seasons were mysterious. Today we can explain what causes these events. But to the Greeks, they seemed like the work of powerful gods.

From *World History*, Ancient Greece

Pick a text feature that interests you.

_____
_____
_____
_____
_____
_____

▼

Ask yourself a question about the text feature.

_____
_____
_____
_____
_____
_____

▼

Set a purpose for your reading.

_____
_____
_____
_____
_____
_____
_____

Setting a Purpose

As you read about geography you will come across a lot of new information. Setting a purpose can help keep you focused and moving toward your goal of understanding.

YOU TRY IT!
Use text features to help you set a purpose that will guide your reading. Complete the graphic organizer to help you through the steps of setting a purpose.

Section 3: East Africa Today

What You Will Learn...
Main Ideas
1. National parks are a major source of income for Tanzania and Kenya.
2. Rwanda and Burundi are densely populated rural countries with a history of ethnic conflict.
3. Both Sudan and Uganda have economies based on agriculture, but Sudan has suffered from years of war.
4. The countries of the Horn of Africa are among the poorest in the world.

The Big Idea
East Africa has abundant national parks, but most of the region's countries are poor and recovering from conflicts.

Building Background
Many of the countries of East Africa are rich in natural resources—including wildlife—but people disagree about the best way to use them. Droughts can make life here difficult. In addition, political and ethnic conflicts have led to unrest and violence in some areas of the region.

From *Africa*, East Africa

Pick a text feature that interests you.
_____
_____
_____
_____
_____
_____

▼

Ask yourself a question about the text feature.
_____
_____
_____
_____
_____
_____

▼

Set a purpose for your reading.
_____
_____
_____
_____
_____
_____

Setting a Purpose

As you read about civics and government you will come across a lot of new information. Setting a purpose can help keep you focused and moving toward your goal of understanding.

YOU TRY IT!
Use text features to help you set a purpose that will guide your reading. Complete the graphic organizer to help you through the steps of setting a purpose.

The President's Roles

The Constitution states that "the executive power shall be vested in [given to] a President of the United States of America. This power applies to several areas of the government, including the military and foreign policy.

Legislative Leader The president recommends, or suggests, new laws to Congress. Every year the president delivers a State of the Union Address to Congress. Usually presented in late January, this televised speech sets forth the programs and policies that the president wants Congress to put into effect as laws. These programs and policies usually address the country's most pressing concerns. The president also sends Congress a budget proposing how the federal government should raise and spend money. In this budget, the president recommends laws and programs to help the economy. The legislature often does not follow the president's budget plan.

The president also influences Congress by indicating what legislation he or she does not want. One powerful way for the president to do this is by using the veto. This tactic is so effective that just the threat of a presidential veto often discourages Congress from passing a bill. It takes a two-thirds vote of both houses of Congress to override a veto, or pass a bill after a president has vetoed it.

From *Civics in Practice*, The Executive Branch

Pick a text feature that interests you.
_____
_____
_____
_____
_____
_____
_____

▼

Ask yourself a question about the text feature.
_____
_____
_____
_____
_____
_____

▼

Set a purpose for your reading.
_____
_____
_____
_____
_____
_____
_____

Have you ever been caught up in a mystery novel or TV show? As you follow the clues, sometimes you can solve the crime before the book or the show ends. When you do that, you are making a prediction, or a guess about what will happen next.

Making predictions can also help you as you read social studies. Predicting helps you to stay involved with your reading as you try to find out whether your prediction was right.

HOW TO MAKE PREDICTIONS

To make predictions, follow these four basic steps:

1. **Rely on information that you already know.** As you read social studies, think of what you already know about people, places, events, and other subjects.

2. **Add new information from your reading.** Your textbook will provide new information that you should consider along with what you already know.

3. **Form a prediction that makes sense.** Put the old and new information together to make a prediction. In social studies, your predictions will focus on what you think might have happened next or what life was like in different cultures or at different times.

4. **Confirm or adjust your prediction.** As you continue reading, you will see how accurate your prediction was. If necessary, you can adjust it and move on to the next prediction.

Physical Features

Eastern Europe is a land of amazing contrasts. The northern parts of the region lie along the cold, often stormy shores of the Baltic Sea. In the south, however, are warm, sunny beaches along the Adriatic and Black seas. Jagged mountain peaks jut high into the sky in some places, while wildflowers dot the gently rolling hills of other parts of the region. These contrasts stem from the region's wide variety of landforms, water features, and climates.

From *Europe and Russia,* Eastern Europe

1. Take what you already know.	2. Add new information from your reading.	3. Form predictions that make sense.	4. Confirm or adjust your prediction.
I know places with warm, sunny beaches are popular with tourists.	There are warm beaches along the Adriatic and Black seas.	The warm beaches of Eastern Europe probably attract many tourists.	Ah ha! A few pages later the textbook says that the region's beaches are popular with tourists.

Making Predictions

Reading Skills

Reading American History

As you read about American history you will come across a lot of new information. Making predictions can help you stay involved with your reading as you see whether your prediction was right.

YOU TRY IT!

Read the following passage about the counterculture of the 1960s. As you read, think about what you already know about teens, rebellion, and hippies. Then predict in what ways the teens and young adults expressed their rebellion.

Rise of the Counterculture

The counterculture of the 1960s was a rebellion of teens and young adults against mainstream American society. These young Americans, called hippies, believed that society's values were hollow and its priorities were misplaced. Turning their backs on the mainstream—which they called the establishment—hippies wanted to create an alternative culture based on peace and love.

Where did the counterculture come from? First of all, the number of teens and young adults in the United States rose dramatically in the 1960s. Between 1960 and 1970 the number of Americans aged 15 through 24 increased almost 50 percent.

From *American Anthem*, A Time of Social Change

What I already know	New information I read	My prediction
_____	_____	_____
_____	_____	_____
_____	_____	_____
_____	_____	_____
_____	_____	_____
_____	_____	_____
_____	_____	_____

Making Predictions

As you read about world history you will come across a lot of new information. Making predictions can help you stay involved with your reading as you see whether your prediction was right.

YOU TRY IT!

Read the following passage about how the church influenced art during the Middle Ages. As you read, think about what you already know about art and religion. Then predict what kind of objects artists might have created during the Middle Ages.

The Church and the Arts

In addition to politics and education, the church was also a strong influence on art and architecture. Throughout the Middle Ages, religious feeling inspired artists and architects to create beautiful works of art.

Religious Architecture Many of Europe's churches were incredible works of art. The grandest of these churches were cathedrals, large churches in which bishops led religious services. Beginning in the 1100s Europeans built their cathedrals using a dramatic new style called Gothic architecture.

Gothic cathedrals were not only places to pray, but also symbols of people's faith. As a result, they were towering works of great majesty and glory.

From *World History*, The Later Middle Ages

What I already know	New information I read	My prediction
_____	_____	_____
_____	_____	_____
_____	_____	_____
_____	_____	_____
_____	_____	_____
_____	_____	_____
_____	_____	_____

Reading Social Studies

Making Predictions

Reading Skills
Reading Geography

As you read about geography you will come across a lot of new information. Making predictions can help you stay involved with your reading as you see whether your prediction was right.

YOU TRY IT!

Read the following passage about population growth in Kenya. As you read, think about what you already know about population growth. Then predict what kinds of challenges Kenya might face because of its population explosion.

Population Growth in Kenya

If the current growth rate continues, the world's population will grow by almost a billion people every 12 years! Countries where big families bring high status and ensure care for elders later in life have the highest growth rates. In addition, farming families often want many children so they can work in the fields. All these factors apply to Kenya. In 1988 Kenya had a population growth rate of 4.2 percent— the highest any country has ever recorded. Kenya's growth rate soared because more children were born, fewer children died, and modern medicine kept more people alive longer.

After Kenya won independence in 1963, the country's economy expanded quickly. However, by the 1980s the economy could no longer keep pace with the population. Too many resources went just to supply the needs of the huge population. Little was left over for development.

From *World Geography Today*, East Africa

What I already know	**New information I read**	**My prediction**
_____	_____	_____
_____	_____	_____
_____	_____	_____
_____	_____	_____
_____	_____	_____
_____	_____	_____
_____	_____	_____

Making Predictions

As you read about civics and government you will come across a lot of new information. Making predictions can help you stay involved with your reading as you see whether your prediction was right.

YOU TRY IT!

Read the following passage about Congress. As you read, think about what you already know about laws that affect your life. Then predict what kinds of laws Congress has the authority to make.

The Powers of Congress

The U.S. Congress is the most powerful representative body in the world. Under the Constitution, Congress's most important responsibility is to make laws. These laws do not simply tell us what we can and cannot do. They affect us in other ways as well. For example, laws passed by Congress determine how high taxes will be. They provide for the building of highways and dams. They determine what military equipment the United States will sell to other countries. The actions of Congress affect the lives of millions of people in the United States and throughout the world.

From *Civics in Practice*, The Legislative Branch

What I already know	New information I read	My prediction
_____	_____	_____
_____	_____	_____
_____	_____	_____
_____	_____	_____
_____	_____	_____
_____	_____	_____

A main idea is like the hub of a wheel. The hub holds the wheel together, and everything circles around it. In a paragraph, the main idea holds the information together. All the facts and details revolve around the main idea.

Why do we bother to look for main ideas? Social studies is not just a bunch of facts. Instead, it is about facts and their meanings. When we find main ideas, we find the meaning behind the details.

HOW TO IDENTIFY MAIN IDEAS AND DETAILS

To identify a main idea and details, follow these three basic steps:

1. **Identify the topic of the paragraph.** Ask yourself, "What is this paragraph mostly about?"

2. **Note important facts and details that relate to the topic.** The details help you understand something about the topic of the paragraph.

3. **Determine the main idea.** The main idea is the main point about the topic. It shapes the paragraph's content and the meaning of all the facts and details in it. Sometimes the main idea is stated clearly in a sentence. Other times the main idea is only suggested, not stated.

City Growth

A number of different factors have influenced the site and growth of cities. One is location near key resources. Other factors include location along transportation and trade routes and at easily defended sites. Many of the world's greatest cities grew up where two or three of these factors were present. Once cities are established, continued access to other cities and resources allows them to grow and prosper.

From *World Geography Today*, Human Systems

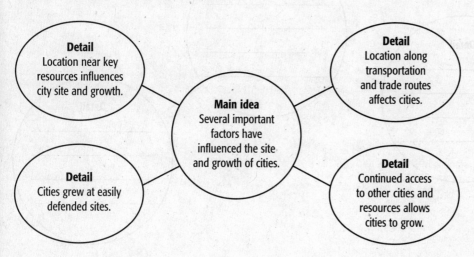

Identifying Main Ideas and Details

As you read about American history you will come across a lot of new
information. To make sure you grasp important points as you read,
practice identifying the main idea and details. That way you will know
you are focusing on the right information.

YOU TRY IT!

Read the following passage. Then fill in the diagram with the main idea
and supporting details. Remember, the main idea might not always be
stated in the paragraph.

Industry Changes Society

Every time motorists turned the crank handle to start their cars,
other industries benefited. Demand for steel, glass, rubber, and other
automobile materials soared. Automobile repair shops and filling
stations sprang up in cities and towns. Motels and restaurants arose
to meet the needs of car travelers.

From *American Anthem*, From War to Peace

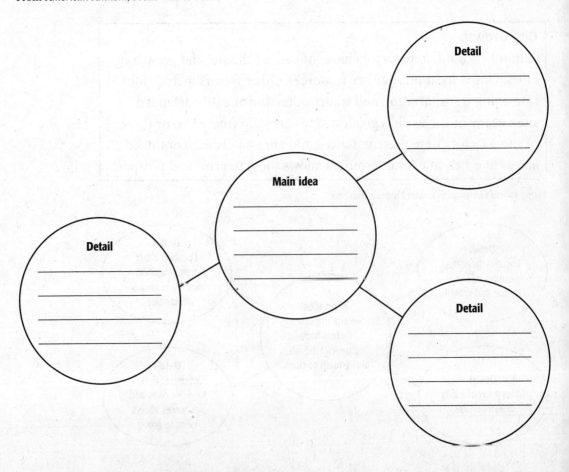

Reading Social Studies

Identifying Main Ideas and Details

Reading Skills
Reading World History

As you read about world history you will come across a lot of new
information. To make sure you grasp important points as you read,
practice identifying the main idea and details. That way you will know
you are focusing on the right information.

YOU TRY IT!

Read the following passage. Then fill in the diagram with the main idea
and supporting details. Remember, the main idea might not always be
stated in the paragraph.

Disorder in the Republic

Rome in the 70s BC was a dangerous place. Politicians and generals
went to war to increase their power even as political order broke
down in Rome. There were politically inspired riots to restore the
power of the tribunes. All the while, more and more people from
throughout the republic flooded into the city, further adding to the
confusion.

From *World History*, Rome and Christianity

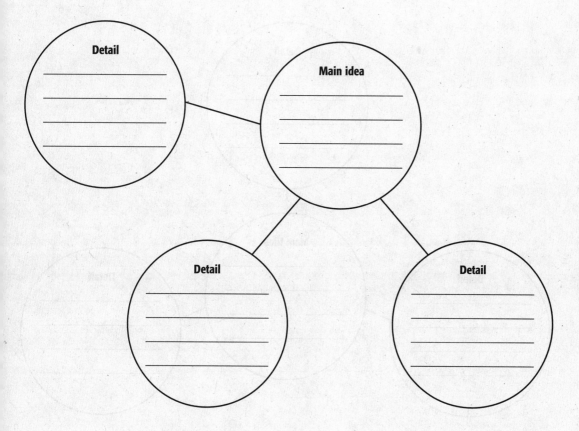

Identifying Main Ideas and Details

As you read about geography you will come across a lot of new information. To make sure you grasp important points as you read, practice identifying the main idea and details. That way you will know you are focusing on the right information.

YOU TRY IT!

Read the following passage. Then fill in the diagram with the main idea and supporting details. Remember, the main idea might not always be stated in the paragraph.

> **Culture**
> Because of their shared history, Ireland and Great Britain share many cultural features. Social life is often centered around local eateries. Sports such as soccer, rugby, and cricket are popular. In addition, English is the main language of both countries. However a small number of Irish also speak Irish Gaelic, and some Scots speak Scottish Gaelic.

From *World Geography Today*, Northern and Western Europe

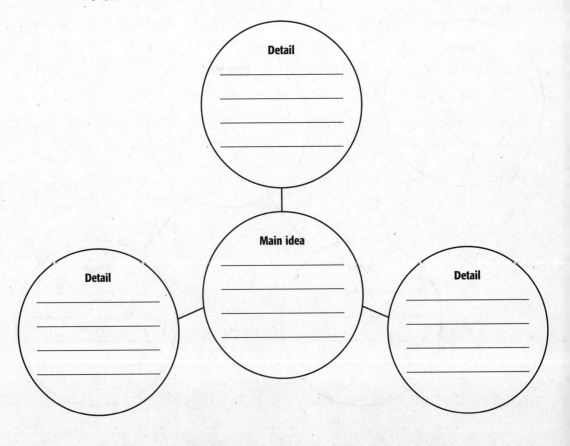

Reading Social Studies

Identifying Main Ideas and Details

Reading Skills

Reading Civics

As you read about civics and government you will come across a lot of new information. To make sure you grasp important points as you read, practice identifying the main idea and details. That way you will know you are focusing on the right information.

YOU TRY IT!

Read the following passage. Then fill in the diagram with the main idea and supporting details. Remember, the main idea might not always be stated in the paragraph.

> **Organization of the House of Representatives**
>
> The person who presides over the House when it is in session is called the Speaker of the House. The Speaker, who is always a member of the majority party, is the most powerful officer in the House. For example, no representative may speak until called on, or recognized, by the Speaker. The Speaker also influences the order of business in the House.

From *Civics in Practice*, The Legislative Branch

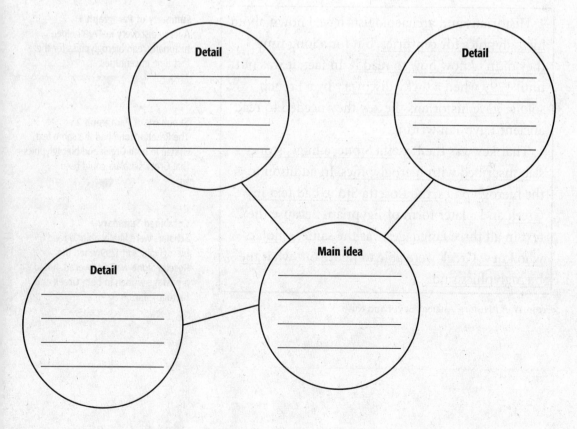

Maybe you have watched a TV commercial and enjoyed the fast-moving pictures, music, and dialogue. Suppose that as you flip through a magazine, you come across the same ad. You see that the TV commercial has been stripped down to the most important details. The magazine ad is a summary of the TV commercial.

As you read social studies, you can use a summary to help you focus on and remember what you read. A summary is like the magazine ad. It is a short restatement, or stripped-down version, of the most important points of the text.

To create a summary, follow three basic steps.

1. **Underline the important details in the passage.** Look for ideas, names, places, and other facts that get right to the meat of the passage.

2. **Write one or two sentences that summarize the important details in the paragraph or passage.** As you summarize, you may realize that you need to delete or add information. Try to make your summary both short and complete.

3. **Combine these paragraph summaries into a short summary of the whole passage.** Try to be as concise as possible, but don't leave out important information. Your summary should jog your memory of the entire passage.

Historians and archaeologists have known about <u>hieroglyphics for centuries</u>, but for a long time <u>they didn't know how to read it</u>. In fact, it was not until <u>1799</u> when <u>a lucky discovery</u> by a French soldier <u>gave historians the key</u> they needed to read ancient Egyptian writing.

That key was the <u>Rosetta Stone, a huge, stone slab inscribed with hieroglyphics</u>. In addition to the hieroglyphics, <u>the Rosetta Stone had text in Greek</u> and a later form of Egyptian. Because the text in all three languages was the same, <u>scholars who knew Greek were able to figure out what the hieroglyphics said</u>.

From *World History*, Ancient Egypt and Kush

Summary of Paragraph 1
A lucky discovery in 1799 helped historians read hieroglyphics for the first time in centuries.

Summary of Paragraph 2
The Rosetta Stone had the same text written in both Greek and hieroglyphics that Greek scholars could read.

Combined Summary
Scholars were finally able to read hieroglyphics in 1799 when the Rosetta Stone was discovered. It had a passage written in both Greek and hierogpyphics.

Summarizing

As you read about American history, you will come across a lot of new information. Summarizing can help you focus on and remember what you read.

YOU TRY IT!

Read the following passage and underline the important points. Then fill out the graphic organizer below to create a summary. The first box has been completed for you.

The Nuremberg Trials

Following World War II, many of the Nazis believed to be responsible for the Final Solution and the concentration camps were put on trial. The court was called the International Military Tribunal. It was organized by the United States, Great Britain, France, and the Soviet Union.

A total of 22 Nazis were tried for war crimes. Included were some of the leading figures of the Nazi movement, including Hermann Goering. Twelve were sentenced to die. Several others served long prison terms.

In addition, following this trial, several other Nazis were captured and tried in different courts. These trials demonstrated the commitment of people around the world to remember the terrible experience of the Jews at the hands of the Nazis—known today as the Holocaust.

From *American Anthem*, The United States in World War II

Summary of Paragraph 1
A trial called the International Military Tribunal was held after World War II to try Nazis for war crimes.

▼

Summary of Paragraph 2
_____
_____
_____
_____

▼

Summary of Paragraph 3
_____
_____
_____
_____

▼

Combined Summary
_____
_____
_____
_____
_____
_____

Reading Social Studies

Summarizing

Reading Skills
Reading World History

As you read about world history you will come across a lot of new information. Summarizing can help you focus on and remember what you read.

YOU TRY IT!

Read the following passage and underline the important points. Then fill out the graphic organizer below to create a summary. The first box has been completed for you.

Scrolls Reveal Past Beliefs
Besides the Torah, the Hebrew Bible, and the Commentaries, many other documents explain ancient Jewish beliefs. Among the most important are the Dead Sea Scrolls, writings by Jews who lived about 2,000 years ago.
Until 1947 no one knew about the Dead Sea Scrolls. In that year, young boys looking for a lost goat near the Dead Sea found a small cave. One of the boys went in to explore and found several old jars filled with moldy scrolls.
Scholars were very excited about the boys' find. Eager to find more scrolls, they began to search the desert. Over the next few decades, searchers found several more groups of scrolls.
Careful study revealed that most of the Dead Sea Scrolls were written between 100 BC and AD 50. The scrolls included prayers, commentaries, letters, and passages from the Hebrew Bible. These writings help historians learn about the lives of many Jews during this time.

From *World History*, The Hebrews and Judaism

Summary of Paragraph 1
The Dead Sea scrolls, which were written 2,000 years ago, help explain ancient Jewish beliefs.

▼

Summary of Paragraph 2
_____
_____
_____

▼

Summary of Paragraph 3
_____
_____
_____

▼

Summary of Paragraph 4
_____
_____
_____

▼

Combined Summary
_____
_____
_____
_____
_____

Reading Social Studies

Summarizing

Reading Skills
Reading Geography

As you read about geography you will come across a lot of new information. Summarizing can help you focus on and remember what you read.

YOU TRY IT!

Read the following passage and underline the important points. Then fill out the graphic organizer below to create a summary. The first box has been completed for you.

The Moscow Region

Moscow, with its huge Kremlin, has symbolized Russia for centuries. The city became the home of the Russian Orthodox Church in the 1300s and Russia's capital in the 1400s. Most Russians have looked to Moscow as their country's heart and soul. This was true even while St. Petersburg was the capital from 1712 to 1918.

Today Greater Moscow is Russia's most important economic region. It is the national center of communications, culture, education, finance, politics, and transportation. More than 70 institutions of higher learning are there. As a result, Moscow's economic advantages are many. Roads, rails, and air routes link the capital to all points in Russia. The city's location also gives its businesses access to raw materials and labor.

The economic region around Moscow stretches for many miles in all directions. Millions of Russians live and work within the area's network of transportation routes and job sites. Among the transportation links is the world's busiest subway. The area also has electrified railroads and a major beltway.

From *World Geography Today*, Russia, Ukraine, and Belorus

Summary of Paragraph 1
Russians love Moscow, the country's capital and religious center.

▼

Summary of Paragraph 2
_____
_____
_____
_____

▼

Summary of Paragraph 3
_____
_____
_____
_____

▼

Combined Summary
_____
_____
_____
_____
_____
_____
_____

Summarizing

As you read about civics and government you will come across a lot of new information. Summarizing can help you focus on and remember what you read.

YOU TRY IT!

Read the following passage and underline the important points. Then fill out the graphic organizer below to create a summary. The first box has been completed for you.

Propaganda and Public Opinion

Many of the ideas in the mass media have been directed at us for a purpose. Someone or some group is urging us to do something—to buy something, to believe something, or to act in a certain way. Ideas that are spread to influence people are called propaganda.

It has been said that we live in the propaganda age. Propaganda is certainly nothing new, but it has become increasingly influential in recent years. Two reasons for this development are the tremendous growth of the mass media and advances in communications technology. Communications satellites, computer networks, and television broadcasts all help spread propaganda farther and faster than ever before.

There are always many people, groups, and advertisers using propaganda to influence public opinion. Advertisers use propaganda to urge consumers to buy their products. Political candidates use propaganda to convince voters to support them.

From *Civics in Practice*, The Political System

Summary of Paragraph 1
The mass media often uses propaganda to influence people to act or believe in a certain way.

▼

Summary of Paragraph 2
_____
_____
_____
_____

▼

Summary of Paragraph 3
_____
_____
_____
_____

▼

Combined Summary
_____
_____
_____
_____
_____
_____

What is the difference between a good guess and a weak guess?
A good guess is an educated guess. In other words, the guess is based
on some knowledge or information. An educated guess is sometimes
called an inference.

Sometimes reading well means understanding what the writer does not
tell you as well as what the writer does tell you. Making inferences can
help you understand and make connections with the text.

HOW TO MAKE INFERENCES

To make inferences, follow these four basic steps:

1. **Ask a question that the text does not directly answer.** Pick a topic that interests
   you. What does the writer not tell you about this topic?

2. **Note information "inside the text."** If you chose a good question, your textbook
   will provide clues to the question.

3. **Note information "outside the text."** Think about what you already know about
   the subject from earlier reading or from your own experience.

4. **Use both sets of information to make an educated guess, or inference.**
   Combine what you read with what you already know. With this full set of information, you should be able to figure out what the writer does not tell you.

Northern Draft

In March 1863, war critics erupted again when
Congress approved a draft, or forced military service. For $300, men were allowed to buy their way
out of military service. For an unskilled laborer,
however, that was nearly a year's wages. Critics of
the draft called the Civil War a "rich man's war and
a poor man's fight."

From *United States History*, The Civil War

---

1. Question
Why were people critical of the draft?

▼

2. Information "inside the text"
- Men could buy their way out
  of military service.
- The fee to get out of military
  service was very high for
  unskilled laborers.
- Critics called it a rich man's war
  and a poor man's fight.

▼

3. Information "outside the text"
- A draft means they were probably
  having a hard time getting people
  to fight.
- $300 was a lot of money back then.

▼

4. Inference
Critics thought the draft was unfair to
poor people.

Making Inferences

Reading Skills
Reading American History

As you read about American history you will come across a lot of new information. Making inferences shows that you can apply your knowledge as you read.

YOU TRY IT!
Read the following passage. Combine information you read with what you already know to make an inference about the earliest battles of the Civil War.

Training the Soldiers
Both the Union and Confederate armies faced shortages of clothing, food, and even rifles. Most troops lacked standard uniforms and simply wore their own clothes. Eventually, each side chose a color for their uniforms. The Union chose blue. The Confederates wore gray.

The problem with volunteers was that many of them had no idea how to fight. Schoolteachers, farmers, and laborers all had to learn the combat basics of marching, shooting, and using bayonets.

With visions of glory and action, many young soldiers were eager to fight. They would not have to wait long.

Discipline and drill were used to turn raw volunteers into an efficient fighting machine. During a battle, the success or failure of a regiment often depended on its discipline—how well it responded to orders.

Volunteers also learned how to use rifles. Eventually, soldiers were expected to be able to load, aim, and fire their rifles three times in one minute. The quality of the weapons provided varied greatly.

From *United States History*, The Civil War

Question
What were the earliest battles of the Civil War probably like?

Information "inside the text"
_____
_____
_____
_____
_____
_____

Information "outside the text"
_____
_____
_____
_____
_____
_____

Inference
_____
_____
_____
_____

Reading Social Studies

Making Inferences

As you read about world history you will come across a lot of new information. Making inferences shows that you can apply your knowledge as you read.

YOU TRY IT!

Read the following passage. Combine information you read with what you already know to make an inference about why the Aryans did not build big cities.

Government and Society

As nomads, the Aryans took along their herds of animals as they moved. But over time, they settled in villages and began to farm. Unlike the Harappans, they did not build big cities.

The Aryan political system was also different from the Harappan system. The Aryans lived in small communities, based mostly on family ties. No single ruling authority existed. Instead, each group had its own leader, often a skilled warrior.

Aryan villages were governed by rajas. A raja was a leader who ruled a village and the land around it. Villagers farmed some of this land for the raja. They used other sections as pastures for their cows, horses, sheep, and goats.

Although many rajas were related, they didn't always get along. Sometimes rajas joined forces before fighting a common enemy. Other times, however, rajas went to war against each other. In fact, Aryan groups fought each other nearly as often as they fought outsiders.

From *World History*, Ancient India

Question
Why did the Aryans not build big cities like the Harappans did?

▼

Information "inside the text"
_____
_____
_____
_____
_____
_____
_____

▼

Information "outside the text"
_____
_____
_____
_____
_____
_____
_____
_____

▼

Inference
_____
_____
_____
_____

Making Inferences

Reading Skills

Reading Geography

As you read about geography you will come across a lot of new information. Making inferences shows that you can apply your knowledge as you read.

YOU TRY IT!

Read the following passage. Combine information you read with what you already know to make an inference about when tourists are most likely to visit Central America and the Caribbean islands.

Climates, Plants, and Animals

Central America and the Caribbean islands extend across the sunny and warm tropical latitudes. Tropical wet and dry climates are typical. Temperatures seldom vary more than 10°F between summer and winter. During winter, high pressure generally brings dry weather. A summer rainy season results when low pressure cells begin to move north across the region. Rain can then be expected almost every afternoon. However, the region's physical features cause this general climate pattern to vary.

From *World Geography Today*, Central America and the Caribbean

Question
What is the busiest season for tourism in Central America and the Caribbean?

▼

Information "inside the text"
_____
_____
_____
_____
_____
_____

▼

Information "outside the text"
_____
_____
_____
_____
_____
_____

▼

Inference
_____
_____
_____
_____

Making Inferences

As you read about civics and government you will come across a lot of new information. Making inferences shows that you can apply your knowledge as you read.

YOU TRY IT!

Read the following passage. Combine information you read with what you already know to make an inference about why governments in some countries might not allow freedom of speech.

Freedom of Speech

"Congress shall make no law . . . abridging (limiting) the freedom of speech." This passage protects the right to express our ideas and opinions openly, as well as to listen to the speech of others. It means that we may talk freely to friends and neighbors or deliver a public speech. Free speech seems perfectly natural to us, but in some countries, free speech is severely limited.

One reason free speech is so important is that it allows us the freedom to criticize our government and government officials. People who live under a totalitarian government can be punished for criticizing their leaders.

There are limits to free-speech rights, however. You may not use your free speech rights in a way that could cause physical harm to others. For example, you do not have the right to yell "Fire!" in a crowded room just for fun. Yelling "Fire!" could cause a panic and get people hurt.

From *Civics in Practice*, Rights and Responsibilities

Question
Why do governments in some countries punish people for criticizing their leaders?

▼

Information "inside the text"
_____
_____
_____
_____
_____
_____

▼

Information "outside the text"
_____
_____
_____
_____
_____
_____
_____

▼

Inference
_____
_____
_____
_____

Sequencing

*Most stories have a beginning, a middle, and an end. The information
you read in your social studies books is no different. Identifying the
correct sequence, or order, of events is important to understanding
what you read.*

As you read your textbook, you may find that you need to identify
a sequence of events in order to understand what really took place.
Developing a sequence chain is a good way to help you identify and
understand the order of events.

HOW TO IDENTIFY SEQUENCE

To put events in sequence, follow these three basic steps:

1. **Look for dates or clue words that signal sequence.** Words such as *first, before,
   then, later, soon, next,* and *finally* give you clues to chronological order.

2. **Identify major events in the sequence.** You do not need to worry about minor
   events or details. Focusing on major events will help you understand their order.

3. **Put events in the correct order.** A sequence chain like the one here might help
   you organize information as you identify sequence.

Western Frontier

Most colonial settlements were located along the
Atlantic coast. Colonial settlers, or pioneers, slowly
moved into the Virginia and Carolina backcountry
and the Ohio River valley.

   Indian leaders like Chief Pontiac opposed
British settlement of this new land. Pontiac's
Rebellion began in May 1763 when his forces
attacked British forts on the frontier. Within one
month, they had destroyed or captured seven forts.
Pontiac then led an attack on Fort Detroit. The
British held out for months.

   British leaders feared that more fighting would
take place on the frontier if colonists kept moving
onto American Indian lands. To avoid more conflict, King George III issued the Proclamation of
1763. This law banned British settlement west of
the Appalachian Mountains. The law also ordered
settlers to leave the upper Ohio River valley.

First
Pioneers began to establish new
settlements on American Indian land.

Next
Pontiac's Rebellion begins when Chief
Pontiac's forces attack British forts in
May 1763.

Next
Pontiac attacks Fort Detroit, where the
British hold out for months.

Last
King George III issues the Proclamation
of 1763, banning British settlement in
the west.

From *United States History,* The English Colonies

Reading Social Studies

Sequencing

As you read about American history you will come across a lot of new information. To understand how events unfolded, you need to be able to identify the order in which they happened—their sequence.

YOU TRY IT!

Read the following passage about the Allies' invasion of Italy. Create a sequence chain describing the major events of the invasion.

On to Italy

The first major step in this assault was the July 1943 invasion of the island of Sicily. Soon after the attack began, Roosevelt and Churchill issued a message to the Italian people asking them "whether they want to die for Mussolini and Hitler or live for Italy and civilization." The Italians chose life. By the end of the month, they had turned against dictator Benito Mussolini and forced him from power. The Allies took Sicily a few weeks later. They planned next to occupy the Italian Peninsula.

Hitler, however, was not going to let the Allies simply march through Italy and into Europe. German forces rushed to stop them.

Despite German resistance, the Allies made steady progress at first. Taking part in the fighting were the Tuskegee Airmen. This was a segregated unit of African Americans, the first ever to receive training as pilots in the U.S. military.

From *American Anthem*, The United States in World War II

First

Next

Next

Last

Reading Social Studies

Sequencing

As you read about world history you will come across a lot of new information. To understand how events unfolded, you need to be able to identify the order in which they happened—their sequence.

YOU TRY IT!

Read the following passage about the Tokugawa shogunate. Create a sequence chain describing the major events in its rise to power in Japan.

Strong Leaders Take Over

Soon new leaders rose to power. They began as local rulers, but these men wanted more power. In the 1500s, each fought to unify all of Japan under his control.

The first such leader was Oda Nobunaga. Oda gave his soldiers guns that had been brought to Japan by Portuguese traders. This was the first time guns had been used in Japan. With these new weapons, Oda easily defeated his opponents.

After Oda died, other leaders continued his efforts to unify Japan. By 1600, one of them, Tokugawa Ieyasu, had conquered his enemies. In 1603 Japan's emperor made Tokugawa shogun. From his capital at Edo—now Tokyo—Tokugawa ruled all of Japan.

Tokugawa's rise to power began the Tokugawa shogunate, or rule by shoguns of the Tokugawa family. Early in this period, which lasted until 1868, Japan traded with other countries and let Christian missionaries live in Japan.

From *World History*, Japan

First

_____
_____
_____
_____
_____

▼

Next

_____
_____
_____
_____
_____

▼

Next

_____
_____
_____
_____
_____

▼

Last

_____
_____
_____
_____
_____

Reading Social Studies

Sequencing

Reading Skills

Reading Geography

As you read about geography you will come across a lot of new information. To understand how events unfolded, you need to be able to identify the order in which they happened—their sequence.

YOU TRY IT!

Read the following passage about the water cycle. Create a sequence chain describing the order of events as water changes form.

The Water Cycle

Water is always moving. As water heats up and cools down, it moves from the planet's surface to the atmosphere, or the mass of air that surrounds Earth. One of the most important processes in nature is the water cycle. The water cycle is the movement of water from Earth's surface to the atmosphere and back.

The sun's energy drives the water cycle. As the sun heats water on Earth's surface, some of that water evaporates, or turns from liquid to gas, or water vapor. Water vapor then rises into the air. As the vapor rises, it cools. The cooling causes the water vapor to condense, or change from a vapor into tiny liquid droplets. These droplets join together to form clouds. If the droplets become heavy enough, precipitation occurs—that is, the water falls back to Earth as rain, snow, sleet, or hail.

When that precipitation falls back to Earth's surface, some of the water is absorbed into the soil as groundwater. Excess water, called runoff, flows over land and collects in streams, rivers, and oceans. Because the water cycle is constantly repeating, it allows us to maintain a fairly constant supply of water on Earth.

From *Introduction to Geography*, Planet Earth

First
_____
_____
_____
_____

▼

Next
_____
_____
_____
_____

▼

Next
_____
_____
_____
_____

▼

Last
_____
_____
_____
_____
_____

Reading Social Studies

Sequencing

As you read about civics and government you will come across a lot of new information. To understand how events unfolded, you need to be able to identify the order in which they happened—their sequence.

YOU TRY IT!

Read the following passage about the Supreme Court. Create a sequence chain describing how the Court makes decisions.

Hearing and Deciding Cases

The Supreme Court hears cases by oral argument. Lawyers for the parties in a case each have 30 minutes to present their arguments. Then the justices spend their time reading written arguments and considering what was said in court. When they are ready to decide a case, they hold a private meeting to vote. Each justice has one vote, and decisions are reached by a simple majority.

Eventually, the justices inform the parties of the court's opinion. An opinion explains the reasoning that led to the decision. The Supreme Court's opinion is binding on all lower courts. Sometimes a justice agrees with the decision of the majority, but for different reasons. In that case, the justice may decide to write a concurring opinion.

In many cases, one or more justices disagree with the majority opinion. These justices may file a dissenting opinion. The dissenting opinion explains why the justice believes the majority opinion is wrong. Although dissenting opinions have no effect on the law, they are still important. Many dissenting opinions have later become the law of the land when the beliefs of society and the opinions of the justices change.

From *Civics in Practice*, The Judicial Branch

First
_____
_____
_____
_____

▼

Next
_____
_____
_____
_____

▼

Next
_____
_____
_____
_____

▼

Last
_____
_____
_____
_____
_____

Reading Social Studies

Maybe you have heard this old riddle: "Which came first, the chicken or the egg?" The riddle is asking if the chicken is a cause or an effect. If the chicken came first, the chicken is a cause. If the egg came first, though, the chicken is an effect. What makes the riddle fun is that both the chicken and the egg could be a cause and an effect.

As you read social studies it is important to identify causes and effects. A cause makes something happen. An effect is what happens as a result of a cause.

HOW TO IDENTIFY CAUSE AND EFFECT

To identify causes and effects, follow these three basic steps:

1. **Look for key words that signal cause.** Words such as *reason, basis, because,* and *as* are often used in a discussion of causes. Sometimes a cause is only implied.

2. **Look for key words that signal effect.** Words and phrases such as *therefore, so, as a result,* and *for that reason* are often used to describe effects.

3. **Check to see if there are multiple causes and effects.** Sometimes one cause will create many effects. Other times one effect will have many causes. It is also possible for a cause to lead to an effect, which is in turn a cause of another effect.

The Monarchy Ends

In 1791, the National Assembly finally completed its constitution. It created a new legislative body, the Legislative Assembly. The constitution allowed the French monarchy to continue, but with severe restrictions on the king's power.

With this development, the king and queen suspected that they were not safe. In June 1791 they disguised themselves and tried to flee Paris. They were recognized, however, and rushed back to the Tuileries palace.

From *World History,* The French Revolution and Napoleon

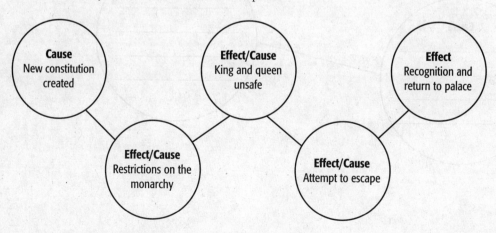

Cause
New constitution created

Effect/Cause
Restrictions on the monarchy

Effect/Cause
King and queen unsafe

Effect/Cause
Attempt to escape

Effect
Recognition and return to palace

Identifying Cause and Effect

Reading Skills

Reading American History

As you read about American history you will come across a lot of new information. You will understand American history better if you learn to recognize causes and effects.

YOU TRY IT!

Read the following passage about changes in the economy. Then fill in the diagram with causes and effect discussed.

> **Weaknesses in the Economy**
> In Florida the wild land boom came to a sudden and disastrous end. Demand for land peaked, then collapsed. Then came "The Big Blow"—the strongest hurricane recorded up to that time. The hurricane had winds of 150 miles per hour, and it killed 243 people. Few people heard the warning on South Florida's only radio station. The hurricane was one of the most destructive ever. As a result, Florida sunk into an economic depression even as other parts of the nation enjoyed prosperity.

From *American Anthem*, From War to Peace

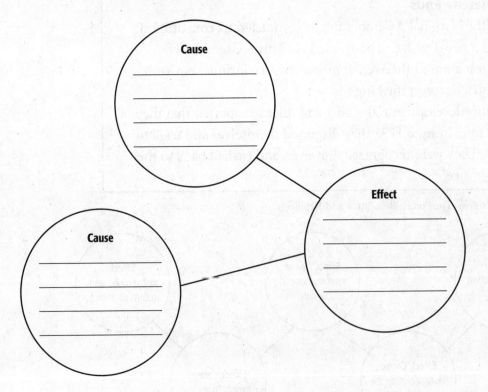

Reading Social Studies

Identifying Cause and Effect　　　　　　　Reading Skills

Reading World History

As you read about world history you will come across a lot of new information. You will understand world history better if you learn to recognize causes and effects.

YOU TRY IT!

Read the following passage about changes in France. Then fill in the diagram with the main cause and the effects it had.

Napoleon's Policies

Napoleon did not just conquer a vast empire. He changed the millions of lives within its borders in several ways.

Many of the changes that Napoleon introduced had widespread impact. Under his leadership, scholars revised and organized French law. Called the Code of Napoleon, this set of laws was adopted by many European governments.

Napoleon learned from France's earlier money troubles that a stable financial system was essential. To avoid such problems in the future, he established the Bank of France. It was privately owned but supervised by the government.

From *World History*, The French Revolution and Napoleon

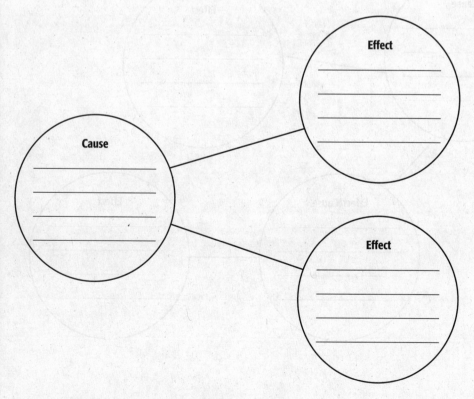

Identifying Cause and Effect　　　　Reading Skills

　　　　　　　　　　　　　　　　　　　　　Reading Geography

As you read about geography you will come across a lot of new information. You will understand geography better if you learn to recognize causes and effects.

YOU TRY IT!

Read the following passage about the Aswan High Dam. Then fill in the diagram with the causes and effects discussed.

Environmental Challenges

Environmental issues in North Africa include desertification, pollution from oil refining, and polluted water supplies. In Egypt the environmental health of the Nile is a major concern. Construction of the Aswan High Dam across the upper Nile was begun in 1960. Once completed, the dam became a major source of hydroelectric power. Water stored behind the dam is used for crops year-round. This water also lets farmers open up new land for farming. These have been important benefits.

From *World Geography Today*, North Africa

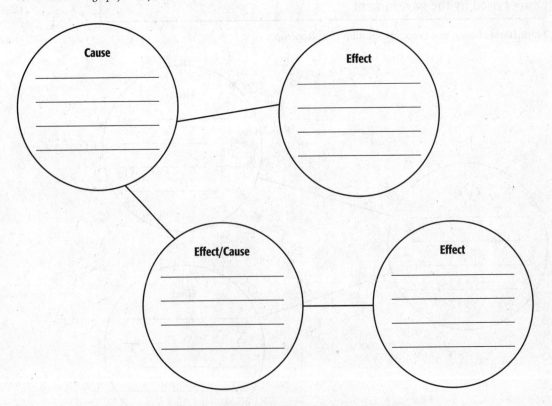

Identifying Cause and Effect

As you read about civics and government you will come across a lot of new information. You will understand civics and government better if you learn to recognize causes and effects.

YOU TRY IT!

Read the following passage about the Second Amendment. Then fill in the diagram with the causes and effect mentioned.

Second Amendment

This amendment was probably created both to ensure that state militias would continue as an armed means of defense and to ensure that individual citizens had a right to own a firearm. Americans in the 1790s had a different attitude toward the military than many people have today. Big national armies were not trusted. Although there had been a regular army in the war for independence, much of the fighting had been done by the state militias. These same militias also defended against attacks from Indians. These concerns led to the Second Amendment, which protects Americans' right to keep and bear arms—that is, to own and carry weapons.

From *Civics in Practice*, Rights and Responsibilities

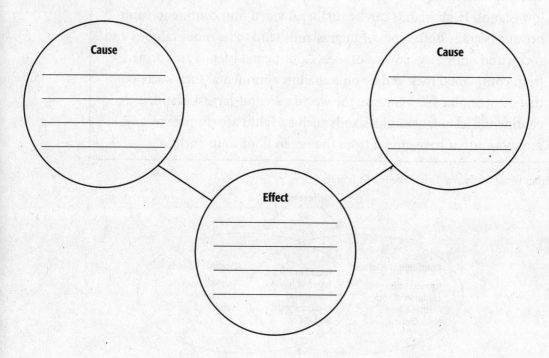

If you have a brother or a sister, you might be used to hearing things like this: "You are so different from your sister," or "You look just like your brother." When people notice how two things are alike they are comparing. When they notice how two things are different they are contrasting.

As you read social studies, comparing and contrasting information can be very useful. Understanding similarities and differences helps you to gain a more complete understanding of what you are reading.

HOW TO COMPARE AND CONTRAST

To compare and contrast, follow these three basic steps:

1. **Identify the two things being compared or contrasted.** Often these will relate to the main topic of the paragraph or section.

2. **Look for clue words.** Words and phrases such as *also, as well as, similarly, same,* and *like* are often used to signal comparison. Words and phrases such as *although, but, different, however,* and *unlike* often signal contrast.

3. **Identify specific similarities and differences.** You may want to use a diagram like the one below to help you identify similarities and differences.

High and Low Islands

Geographers classify the islands of the Pacific as either high islands or low islands. High islands can be further divided into continental and oceanic islands. Both types of high islands tend to be mountainous and rocky, and both may have volcanoes. Continental islands are formed from continental rock and lie on a shallow continental shelf such as that of Australia. New Guinea, the world's second-largest island, is a continental island. Oceanic islands such as Tahiti are simply volcanic mountains that have grown from the ocean floor to its surface.

From *World Geography Today*, The Pacific Islands

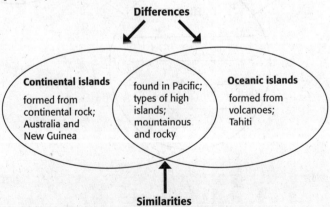

Differences

Continental islands
formed from continental rock; Australia and New Guinea

found in Pacific; types of high islands; mountainous and rocky

Oceanic islands
formed from volcanoes; Tahiti

Similarities

Comparing and Contrasting

Reading Skills
Reading American History

As you read about American history you will come across a lot of new information. You will understand American history better if you learn to compare and contrast information.

YOU TRY IT!

Read the following passage about presidents Roosevelt and Taft. Then fill in the diagram with their similarities and differences.

Progressivism under Taft

Theodore Roosevelt hoped that his secretary of war, William Howard Taft, would take his place as president in 1908. Like Roosevelt, Taft favored business regulation and opposed socialism. With Roosevelt's assistance, Taft defeated William Jennings Bryan in the election of 1908.

Despite their friendship, Roosevelt and Taft held different ideas about how a president should act. Taft thought Roosevelt had claimed more power than a president was constitutionally allowed.

As president, therefore, Taft chose to move cautiously toward reform and regulation. This upset Roosevelt and various Progressives, who supported stricter regulation of big business. Although Taft's administration started twice as many antitrust lawsuits as Roosevelt's had, Progressives were not satisfied.

From *American Anthem*, The Progressives

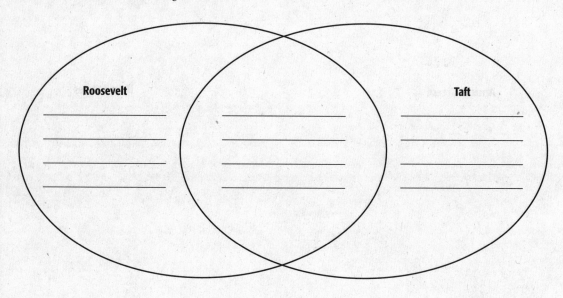

Comparing and Contrasting

Reading Skills

Reading World History

As you read about world history you will come across a lot of new information. You will understand world history better if you learn to compare and contrast information.

YOU TRY IT!

Read the following passage about ancient democracy in Greece and modern democracy in the United States. Then fill in the diagram with their similarities and differences.

Ancient Democracy Differs from Modern Democracy

Like ancient Athens, the Unites States has a democratic government in which the people hold power. But our modern democracy is very different from the ancient Athenians' democracy.

All citizens in Athens could participate directly in the government. We call this form of government a direct democracy. It is called direct democracy because each person's decision directly affects the outcome of a vote. In Athens, citizens gathered together to discuss issues and vote on them. Each person's vote counted, and the majority ruled.

The United States is too large for direct democracy to work for the whole country. For example, it would be impossible for all citizens to gather in one place for a debate. Instead, the founders of the United States set up another kind of democracy.

From *World History*, Ancient Greece

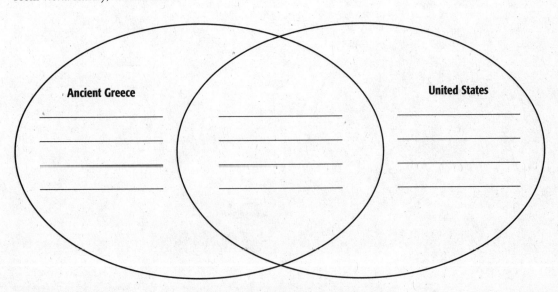

Comparing and Contrasting

Reading Skills
Reading Geography

As you read about geography you will come across a lot of new information. You will understand geography better if you learn to compare and contrast information.

YOU TRY IT!

Read the following passage about the Rhine and Danube rivers. Then fill in the diagram with their similarities and differences.

Water

The Rhine and Danube stand out among Europe's most important rivers. Many cities and industrial areas line their banks, and barges carry goods along their courses. The Rhine rises in the Swiss Alps. It then flows northwestward through Germany and the Netherlands before entering the North Sea. The Danube begins in the uplands of southern Germany. It flows eastward through nine countries in central and eastern Europe. It empties into the Black Sea. Unfortunately, large amounts of pollution enter the ocean from these and other rivers. Cleaning up and controlling pollution in Europe's rivers is a major environmental challenge.

From *World Geography Today*, Natural Environments of Europe

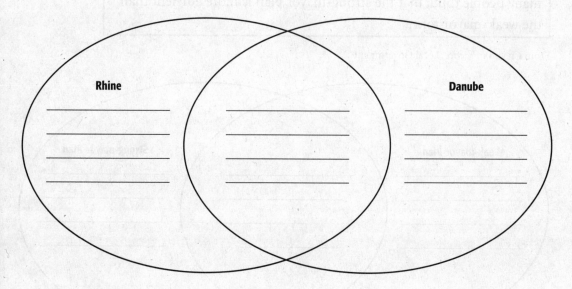

Comparing and Contrasting

Reading Skills

Reading Civics

As you read about civics and government you will come across a lot of new information. You will understand civics and government better if you learn to compare and contrast information.

YOU TRY IT!

Read the following passage about different forms of city government. Then fill in the diagram with their similarities and differences.

Forms of City Government

Under the weak-mayor plan, the city council holds more power than the mayor. For example, the council appoints the city department heads, who report directly to the city council rather than to the mayor. The weak-mayor plan often results in conflicts between the council and the mayor.

Recently, many city governments using the mayor-council form of government have adopted a strong-mayor plan of city government. Under the strong-mayor plan, the mayor is the city's chief executive officer and has the primary responsibility for running the city's government. For example, the mayor appoints most of the city officials . . . Because executive power is concentrated in the mayor, many people think that the strong-mayor plan is more efficient than the weak-mayor form.

From *Civics in Practice*, Local Government

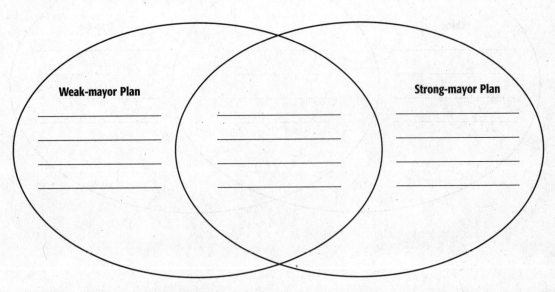

Reading Social Studies

Maybe you have heard the common saying, "When life gives you lemons, make lemonade." In other words, when life gives you a problem, work to find a good solution.

As you read social studies, you will learn about how different people and countries have solved problems. Learning to identify these problems and their solutions as you read will help you understand the information better.

HOW TO IDENTIFY PROBLEMS AND SOLUTIONS

To identify problems and solutions, follow these three basic steps:

1. **Recognize the problem.** Anytime you read about a conflict, crisis, or need, you are reading about a problem. Make sure you know exactly what the problem is, whom it affects, and why it is a problem.

2. **Look for the solution.** Sometimes only one solution is discussed in the text. Other times, you may read about several solutions to the same problem.

3. **Describe the outcome.** Did an attempted solution solve the problem? Or did it fail? Sometimes the text will describe and evaluate the outcome of the solution. Other times, you should try to evaluate on your own whether or not the solution was a good one.

Health

· Like war, disease kills many people in the region. Malaria is a disease spread by mosquitoes that causes fever and pain. Without treatment it can lead to death. In fact, malaria is by far the most common cause of death in Central Africa. A child there dies from malaria every 30 seconds . . .

International health organizations and some national governments have begun to implement strategies to control malaria. These strategies include educating people about the disease and passing out nets treated with insecticide. The nets and medicine are expensive, and not everyone can afford them. However, people who sleep under these nets will be protected from mosquitoes and malaria.

From *Africa*, Central Africa

1. Recognize a problem.
Malaria, a disease spread by mosquitoes, kills many people in Central Africa.

▼

2. Look for the solution.
International health organizations and national governments have begun educating people about how to control the disease and passing out nets treated with insecticide.

▼

3. Describe the outcome.
Solutions are stopping the disease, but only where people can afford medicine and nets.

Identifying Problems and Solutions

Reading Skills

Reading American History

As you read about American history you will come across a lot of new information. Sometimes you will read about problems people and countries have faced. Identifying these problems and their solutions will help you get a better understanding of history.

YOU TRY IT!

Read the following passage. Then complete the graphic organizer to help you identify a problem, its solution, and the outcome.

Inflation and Price Controls

A particular worry was the high rate of inflation, or the overall rise in prices. In the months leading up to the 1972 election, this stood at an unacceptable five percent, and it was rising. Unemployment was also at an uncomfortably high level.

Nixon had traditionally favored limited government involvement in the economy. Now, however, he was willing to take action. In August 1971, he announced a 90-day freeze in wages and prices. That is, businesses could not increase the prices they charged for their products or the wages they paid their workers. This, Nixon hoped, would act as a brake on inflation.

The immediate impact of Nixon's measures was positive. Inflation did appear to slow, at least for a while. Nixon seemed to have successfully addressed a major economic concern of the voters.

Unfortunately, Nixon had not solved the problem of inflation permanently. The oil crisis of 1973–1974 would soon send prices sharply higher again. The wage and price controls that had worked in 1971 failed to bring relief.

From *American Anthem*, A Search for Order

Problem
_____
_____
_____
_____
_____

▼

Solution
_____
_____
_____
_____
_____

▼

Outcome
_____
_____
_____
_____
_____
_____
_____

Reading Social Studies

Identifying Problems and Solutions

Reading Skills
Reading World History

As you read about world history you will come across a lot of new information. Sometimes you will read about problems people and countries have faced. Identifying these problems and their solutions will help you get a better understanding of history.

YOU TRY IT!

Read the following passage. Then complete the graphic organizer to help you identify a problem, its solution, and the outcome.

Written Laws Keep Order

Rome's officials were responsible for making the city's laws and making sure that people followed them. At first these laws weren't written down. The only people who knew all the laws were the patricians who had made them.

Many people were unhappy with this situation. They did not want to be punished for breaking laws they didn't even know existed. As a result, they began to call for Rome's laws to be written down and made accessible to everybody.

Rome's first written law code was produced in 450 BC on 12 bronze tables, or tablets. These tables were displayed in the Forum, Rome's public meeting place. Because of how it was displayed, this code was called the Law of the Twelve Tables.

Over time, Rome's leaders passed many new laws. Throughout their history, though, the Romans looked to the Law of the Twelve Tables as a symbol of Roman law and of their rights as Roman citizens.

From *World History*, The Roman Republic

Problem
_____
_____
_____
_____
_____
_____

▼

Solution
_____
_____
_____
_____
_____
_____

▼

Outcome
_____
_____
_____
_____
_____
_____
_____

Identifying Problems and Solutions

As you read about geography you will come across a lot of new information. Sometimes you will read about problems people and countries have faced. Identifying these problems and their solutions will help you get a better understanding of geography.

YOU TRY IT!

Read the following passage. Then complete the graphic organizer to help you identify a problem, its solution, and the outcome.

The Region Today

Estonia, Latvia, Lithuania, and Poland all still feel the effects of decades of Soviet rule. The economies of all four countries suffered because the Soviets did not build a decent infrastructure. An infrastructure is the set of resources, like roads, airports, and factories, that a country needs in order to support economic activities. The many factories built by the Soviets in Poland and the Baltics could not produce as many goods as those in Western Europe.

Today Poland and the Baltic Republics are working to rebuild and strengthen their economies. They are replacing the old and outdated factories built by the Soviets with new ones that take advantage of modern technology. As a result, cities like Warsaw, the capital of Poland, have become major industrial centers.

To further their economic growth, the countries of this region are also seeking new sources of income. One area in which they have found some success is tourism. Since the collapse of the Soviet Union in 1991, many Americans and Western Europeans have begun visiting. Polish cities like Warsaw and Krakow have long attracted tourists with their rich history and famous sites.

From *Europe and Russia*, Eastern Europe

Problem

_____
_____
_____
_____
_____
_____

▼

Solution

_____
_____
_____
_____
_____
_____

▼

Outcome

_____
_____
_____
_____
_____
_____
_____

Reading Social Studies

Identifying Problems and Solutions

Reading Skills
Reading Civics

As you read about civics and government you will come across a lot of new information. Sometimes you will read about problems people and countries have faced. Identifying these problems and their solutions will help you get a better understanding of government.

YOU TRY IT!

Read the following passage. Then complete the graphic organizer to help you identify a problem, its solution, and the outcome.

Writing the Constitution

The delegates discussed many ideas and proposals for organizing the federal system. They eventually settled many differences of opinion by a series of compromises. A compromise is an agreement in which each side gives up part of its demands in order to reach a solution to a problem.

The most serious disagreement arose over the question of representation in the new national legislature, or lawmaking body. The larger states favored a legislature in which representation would be based on the size of a state's population. The smaller states wanted each state to have an equal number of representatives in the legislature.

Finally, both sides agreed to a compromise. Their agreement provided for a bicameral lawmaking body called Congress. In one house, the Senate, the states were to have equal representation. In the other house, the House of Representatives, each state was to be represented according to the size of its population. This agreement became known as the Great Compromise.

From *Civics in Practice*, Foundations of Government

Problem
_____
_____
_____
_____
_____
_____
_____

▼

Solution
_____
_____
_____
_____
_____
_____
_____

▼

Outcome
_____
_____
_____
_____
_____
_____
_____

Have you ever read a mystery story in which a detective puts together various clues to solve a puzzling crime? In other words, the detective combines various bits of information to reach a conclusion.

A conclusion is a judgment someone makes by combining information. When you read, you can put together various bits of information from what you are reading to figure out new information that is not exactly stated in the text. Drawing conclusions will make you a better reader.

HOW TO DRAW CONCLUSIONS

To draw conclusions, follow these three basic steps:

1. **Read the text to understand the topic.** It is a good idea to read the text looking for clues, even if you do not know yet where they will lead you.

2. **Ask a question that the text does not directly answer.** After you have read the text, think of a question that is related to the information but not directly answered in the text.

3. **Put together clues, or information in the text, to answer the question.** Think back over the information in the text to see if it leads you to discover, or draw a conclusion about, the answer to your question.

The Pyramids

Egyptians believed that burial sites, especially royal tombs, were very important. As a result, they built spectacular monuments in which to bury their rulers. The most spectacular of all were the pyramids, huge stone tombs with four triangle-shaped walls that met in a point on top.

The Egyptians began to build pyramids during the Old Kingdom. Some of the largest pyramids ever constructed were built during this time. Many of these huge structures are still standing. The largest is the Great Pyramid of Khufu near the town of Giza. It covers more than 13 acres at its base and stands 481 feet high. This single pyramid took more than 2 million limestone blocks to build.

From *World History*, Ancient Egypt and Kush

Question
Who was Khufu?

▼

Information from the text
- Egyptians built spectacular monuments in which to bury their rulers.
- The pyramids were tombs.
- The largest pyramid is named after Khufu.

▼

Conclusion
Khufu was an important ruler of Egypt.

Name ______________________ Class ______________ Date __________

Drawing Conclusions

Reading Skills

Reading American History

As you read about American history you will come across a lot of new information. Drawing conclusions helps you put together information to get a more complete understanding of the text.

YOU TRY IT!

Read the following passage. Then put together information from the passage to draw a conclusion about the question in the graphic organizer.

Maryland

In 1634 a group of 200 English Catholics came to Maryland. Included in the group were wealthy landowners, servants, craftspeople, and farmers. Settlers in Maryland benefited from the lessons learned by the Jamestown colonists. They spent their time raising corn, cattle, and hogs so that they would have enough to eat. Before long, many colonists also began growing tobacco for profit.

Although Catholics founded Maryland, a growing number of Protestants began moving there in the 1640s. Soon, religious conflicts arose between Catholics and Protestants in the colony. To reduce tensions, Lord Baltimore presented a bill to the colonial assembly that became known as the Toleration Act of 1649. This bill made it a crime to restrict the religious rights of Christians. This was the first law supporting religious tolerance passed in the English colonies.

From *United States History,* The English Colonies

Question
What was Lord Baltimore's view of religion?

Information from the text

____

____

____

____

____

____

____

____

____

____

Conclusion

____

____

____

____

____

____

Name ______________________ Class ____________ Date ____________

Drawing Conclusions

Reading Skills

Reading World History

As you read about world history you will come across a lot of new information. Drawing conclusions helps you put together information to get a more complete understanding of the text.

YOU TRY IT!

Read the following passage. Then put together information from the passage to draw a conclusion about the question in the graphic organizer.

The Revival of the Family

Since Confucianism was the official government philosophy during Wudi's reign, Confucian teachings about the family were also honored. Children were taught from birth to respect their elders. Disobeying one's parents was a crime. Even emperors had a duty to respect their parents.

Confucius had taught that the father was the head of the family. Within the family, the father had absolute power. The Han taught that it was a woman's duty to obey her husband, and children had to obey their father.

Han officials believed that if the family was strong and people obeyed the father, then people would obey the emperor, too. Since the Han stressed strong family ties and respect for elders, some men even gained government jobs based on the respect they showed their parents.

Children were encouraged to serve their parents. They were also expected to honor dead parents with ceremonies and offerings. All family members were expected to care for family burial sites.

From *World History*, Ancient China

Question
How did the ancient Chinese view Emperor Wudi?

Information from the text

____

____

____

____

____

____

____

____

____

____

Conclusion

____

____

____

____

____

____

Drawing Conclusions

Reading Skills

Reading Geography

As you read about geography you will come across a lot of new information. Drawing conclusions helps you put together information to get a more complete understanding of the text.

YOU TRY IT!

Read the following passage. Then put together information from the passage to draw a conclusion about the question in the graphic organizer.

Water

The main water sources in southern Central Asia are the Syr Darya and Amu Darya rivers. Since water is so scarce there, different ideas over how to use the water from these rivers have led to conflict between Uzbekistan and Turkmenistan.

Today farmers use river water mostly to irrigate cotton fields. Cotton grows well in Central Asia's sunny climate, but it requires a lot of water. Irrigation has taken so much water from the rivers that almost no water actually reaches the Aral Sea today. The effect of this irrigation has been devastating to the Aral Sea. It has lost more than 75 percent of its water since 1960. Large areas of seafloor are now exposed.

In addition to water for irrigation, Central Asia's rivers supply power. Some countries have built large dams on the rivers to generate hydroelectricity.

From *Southwest and Central Asia*, Central Asia

Question
What different views might people in Uzbekistan and Turkmenistan have about the use of water from the Syr Darya and Amu Darya?

▼

Information from the text

_____
_____
_____
_____
_____
_____
_____
_____

▼

Conclusion

_____
_____
_____
_____
_____
_____

Drawing Conclusions

Reading Skills

Reading Civics

As you read about civics and government you will come across a lot of new information. Drawing conclusions helps you put together information to get a more complete understanding of the text.

YOU TRY IT!

Read the following passage. Then put together information from the passage to draw a conclusion about the question in the graphic organizer.

Import Taxes

The U.S. government collects taxes on many products imported from foreign countries. This import tax is called a tariff, or sometimes a customs duty. At one time customs duties were the main source of revenues for the federal government. For example, in 1850 about 90 percent of the federal budget came from customs duties.

Today the United States uses tariffs primarily to regulate foreign trade rather than to raise money. For example, tariffs can be used to raise the prices of imported goods. Tariffs make goods from other countries either as expensive or more expensive than American-made products. In this way tariffs can protect American industry from unfair competition from foreign industry. On the other hand, tariffs can also hurt American consumers by raising the prices of certain products. Using tariffs as a way to control trade, rather than as a source of revenue, is often a difficult balancing act.

From *Civics in Practice*, Paying for Government

Question
What would happen if the government drastically lowered tariffs?

▼

Information from the text

_____
_____
_____
_____
_____
_____
_____
_____
_____

▼

Conclusion

_____
_____
_____
_____
_____
_____

Reading Social Studies

Maybe you have heard someone say, "Girls like dolls," or "Boys like trucks." What do you think of those statements? They are probably true in general, but they are not true for all girls and boys, or course. Statements like those are called generalizations.

A generalization is a broad, general conclusion drawn from several examples or pieces of evidence. As you read social studies, practice making generalizations about the text. Doing so will help you focus on the main points of your reading.

HOW TO MAKE GENERALIZATIONS

To make generalizations, follow these three basic steps:

1. **Note details or examples related to a particular topic in the text.** Often an author will provide several examples to make a main point.

2. **Make a broad statement based on examples or evidence.** Information in the text should lead you to a general conclusion about the topic.

3. **Check that your generalization is valid.** Your statement should allow for exceptions. Some words you can use to show there may be exceptions to your statement are *most, some, often,* and *generally.* Watch out for generalizations that try to apply one idea to every person or situation.

Finding Work

Immigrants with skills that were in demand sometimes found work outside factories and sweatshops. For example, some immigrants worked as bakers, carpenters, masons, or skilled machinists. Others saved or borrowed money to open small businesses such as laundries, barbershops, or street vending carts. New immigrants often opened the same types of businesses in which other immigrants from the same country were already succeeding. They worked hard for long hours to become successful themselves.

From *United States History*, Immigrants and Urban Life

Details or examples from the text
- Skilled immigrants found work in many industries.
- Immigrants opened small businesses.
- New immigrants worked hard for long hours.

Generalization
Immigrants contributed to the economy in many ways.

Making Generalizations

As you read about American history you will come across a lot of new information. Making generalizations will help you sort through the details and focus on the main points of the text.

YOU TRY IT!

Read the following passage. Then use the graphic organizer below to make a generalization. Be sure to check that your generalization is valid and applies to different situations.

Cold War Policies

The United States quickly developed a new foreign policy to deal with the Cold War. It was based on the goal of containment, or preventing the Soviet Union from expanding its influence around the world.

In 1945 the Soviet Union began demanding control over areas in the Mediterranean Sea that were under Turkish authority. In 1946 Communist rebels in Greece threatened to topple the Greek monarchy. At Truman's request, Congress passed an aid package worth millions of dollars for Greece and Turkey. The money, the president said, would "support free peoples who are resisting attempted subjugation [conquest] by armed minorities or outside pressures." U.S. aid helped the Greek army defeat the Communist rebels and protected Turkey from Soviet expansion. This policy of providing aid to help foreign countries fight communism became known as the Truman Doctrine.

From *United States History*, Early Years of the Cold War

Details or examples from the text	Generalization
_____	_____
_____	_____
_____	_____
_____	_____
_____	_____
_____	_____
_____	_____
_____	_____

Making Generalizations

As you read about world history you will come across a lot of new information. Making generalizations will help you sort through the details and focus on the main points of the text.

YOU TRY IT!

Read the following passage. Then use the graphic organizer below to make a generalization. Be sure to check that your generalization is valid and applies to different situations.

Napoleon's Rise to Power

By the summer of 1793, Robespierre and the Jacobins ruled France. Their control was incomplete, however. For example, royalists had let British troops occupy the port city of Toulon. Robespierre sent young Captain Napoleon Bonaparte to remove the royalists and their British supporters. He succeeded within 48 hours.

A year later, Bonaparte had another dazzling victory in Italy over Austrian troops. Then in 1795 he again faced off against rebellious French citizens. A mob was charging the Tuileries palace, so Bonaparte used artillery to shoot into the crowd. Some 200 people were killed, but the survivors fled. Bonaparte, now a general, was put in charge of defending the French interior. He was only 26 years old.

The young general continued to win battles against Italian and Austrian troops and to claim territory for France. He was a brilliant strategist, and his troops could strike quickly because they did not travel with a big supply train. Instead, they took the food they needed from the countryside.

From *World History*, The French Revolution and Napoleon

Details or examples from the text	Generalization
_____	_____
_____	_____
_____	_____
_____ ▶	_____
_____	_____
_____	_____
_____	_____

Making Generalizations

As you read about geography you will come across a lot of new information. Making generalizations will help you sort through the details and focus on the main points of the text.

YOU TRY IT!

Read the following passage. Then use the graphic organizer below to make a generalization. Be sure to check that your generalization is valid and applies to different situations.

Greater Mexico City

Greater Mexico City includes the capital and about 50 smaller cities near it. With a population of more than 19 million, Mexico City is the world's second-largest city and one of the most densely populated urban areas. Thousands of people move there every year looking for work.

While this region does provide job and educational opportunities not so easily found in the rest of the country, its huge population causes problems. For example, Mexico City is very polluted. Factories and cars release exhaust and other pollutants into the air. The surrounding mountains trap the resulting smog—a mixture of smoke, chemicals, and fog. Smog can cause health problems like eye irritation and breathing difficulties.

Another problem that comes from crowding is poverty. Wealth and poverty exist side by side in Mexico City. The city has large urban slums. The slums often exist right next to modern office building, apartments, museums, or universities.

From *The Americas*, Mexico

Details or examples from the text		Generalization
_____		_____
_____		_____
_____		_____
_____	▶	_____
_____		_____
_____		_____
_____		_____

Reading Social Studies

Making Generalizations

Reading Skills
Reading Civics

As you read about civics and government you will come across a lot of new information. Making generalizations will help you sort through the details and focus on the main points of the text.

YOU TRY IT!

Read the following passage. Then use the graphic organizer below to make a generalization. Be sure to check that your generalization is valid and applies to different situations.

Private Financing

Voters, business groups, labor unions, and many other organizations contribute money to the political party that they believe best represents their interests. However, people often worry that big contributors to a candidate will receive special favors if he or she wins. To limit political contributions, Congress passed the Federal Election Campaign Act (FECA) in 1972. In 2002, Congress passed the Bipartisan Campaign Reform Act (BCRA), which revised the contribution limits.

The BCRA requires every political candidate in federal elections to report the name of each person who contributes $200 or more in a year. The law limits individual contributions to candidates to $2,100 for primary elections and another $2,100 for general elections. The Federal Election Commission enforces these laws.

From *Civics in Practice*, The Citizen in Government

Details or examples from the text	Generalization
_____	_____
_____	_____
_____	_____
_____	_____
_____	_____
_____	_____
_____	_____
_____	_____
_____	_____

Reading Social Studies

How to Use Think-Alouds with Your Students

OVERVIEW

It happens all the time. You ask students to tell you something about what they've read, and they meet your request with blank stares. They seem to know nothing about the text, but they maintain they've read it. Many of these students have done what they consider reading: Their eyes have traveled over the words from left to right and from top to bottom, and they've turned pages at the appropriate time. What they haven't done is pay any attention to what those words mean; they haven't been thinking about what they are reading. That's when a strategy called Think-Aloud can help.

Think-Alouds are dialogues with the text. A student reads a passage and makes comments about it while a partner listens and identifies the types of comments on a tally sheet. Types of comments include predicting, picturing the text, making comparisons, identifying problems, fixing problems, and making general comments. Eventually, after students have internalized this strategy, they will learn to monitor their comprehension by silently maintaining a dialogue with the text.

MODELING THINK-ALOUDS

- Tell students that the Think-Aloud strategy helps them to monitor comprehension of the texts they read. Explain that when students use Think-Alouds, they are pausing to make different types of comments about the text as they read.

- Review the possible types of Think-Aloud comments that students will be making. Pass out the handout on Types of Think-Aloud Comments.

> - predicting what happens next ("I bet that . . .")
>
> - picturing the text ("I can see that . . .")
>
> - making comparisons ("This sounds like . . .")
>
> - identifying and fixing problems in understanding ("What does this mean? Maybe it means . . .")
>
> - connecting to what they already know ("This reminds me of . . .")
>
> - making comments ("I like this part because . . .")
>
> - questioning what is happening in the text ("I wonder why . . .")

- Then, read one of the model selections in this workbook, pausing to make the Think-Aloud comments that correspond with the numbers in the selection. Be sure the students can tell when you are reading the text and when you are "thinking aloud." You may also want to pass out the models. Have students cover up the "Comments" side and follow along as you read.

- As you make each comment or after you read the whole selection, discuss with the students the different types of comments you made.

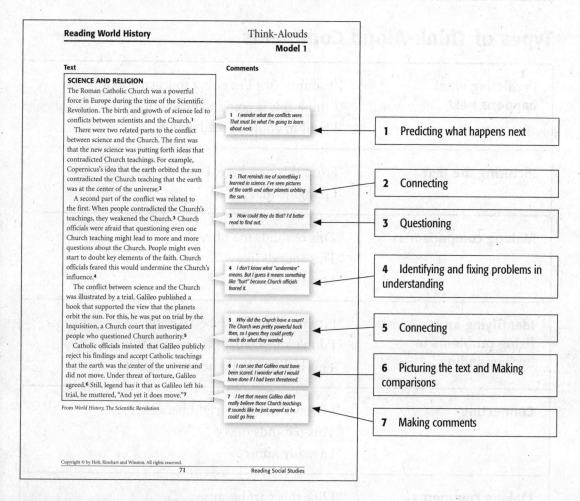

Reading World History   Think-Alouds
                                                  Model 1

Text   **Comments**

SCIENCE AND RELIGION
The Roman Catholic Church was a powerful force in Europe during the time of the Scientific Revolution. The birth and growth of science led to conflicts between scientists and the Church.[1]

There were two related parts to the conflict between science and the Church. The first was that the new science was putting forth ideas that contradicted Church teachings. For example, Copernicus's idea that the earth orbited the sun contradicted the Church teaching that the earth was at the center of the universe.[2]

A second part of the conflict was related to the first. When people contradicted the Church's teachings, they weakened the Church.[3] Church officials were afraid that questioning even one Church teaching might lead to more and more questions about the Church. People might even start to doubt key elements of the faith. Church officials feared this would undermine the Church's influence.[4]

The conflict between science and the Church was illustrated by a trial. Galileo published a book that supported the view that the planets orbit the sun. For this, he was put on trial by the Inquisition, a Church court that investigated people who questioned Church authority.[5]

Catholic officials insisted that Galileo publicly reject his findings and accept Catholic teachings that the earth was the center of the universe and did not move. Under threat of torture, Galileo agreed.[6] Still, legend has it that as Galileo left his trial, he muttered, "And yet it does move."[7]

From *World History*, The Scientific Revolution

1 *I wonder what the conflicts were. That must be what I'm going to learn about next.*

2 *That reminds me of something I learned in science. I've seen pictures of the earth and other planets orbiting the sun.*

3 *How could they do that? I'd better read to find out.*

4 *I don't know what "undermine" means. But I guess it means something like "hurt" because Church officials feared it.*

5 *Why did the Church have a court? The Church was pretty powerful back then, so I guess they could pretty much do what they wanted.*

6 *I can see that Galileo must have been scared. I wonder what I would have done if I had been threatened.*

7 *I bet that means Galileo didn't really believe those Church teachings. It sounds like he just agreed so he could go free.*

1 Predicting what happens next

2 Connecting

3 Questioning

4 Identifying and fixing problems in understanding

5 Connecting

6 Picturing the text and Making comparisons

7 Making comments

71   Reading Social Studies

PRACTICE FOR YOUR STUDENTS

- Remind students that making comments about what they are reading as they read will help them to stay focused on the text and monitor their understanding.

- Make sure students have the handout on Types of Think-Aloud Comments, and assign a passage from the textbook for students to read.

- Have students pair up with a partner. One student will be the designated reader; the other will be the designated listener. The reader should begin reading from the textbook, pausing to make comments. The listener should use his or her own paper to jot down the comments the reader makes. Halfway through, the partners should switch roles.

> **Tip** If students have a very difficult time, you can scaffold this practice by telling them exactly where you want them to stop and comment. You can even tell them that after they read a particular section, they are to describe the scene they see (picturing the text) or discuss how this relates to something they already know (connecting).

- When students finish reading and commenting, have them refer to the Types of Think-Alouds Comments handout and discuss with their partners the different types of comments they made.

Types of Think-Aloud Comments

Predicting what happens next	"It sounds like I'm going to learn about . . ." "I think this is going to be about . . ." "I bet I'm going to read about . . ."
Picturing the text	"From this part here, I can see that . . ." "I imagine that . . ."
Making comparisons	"This reminds me of . . ." "This sounds like . . ." "This is similar to . . ."
Identifying and fixing problems in understanding	"I don't get this. Maybe I'd better . . ." "I don't know what this means. What if . . ." "This is difficult. I'd better consider . . ."
Connecting	"I know this part is right because . . ." "This reminds me of . . ." "I already know . . ."
Making comments	"I like this part because . . ." "I think this means that . . ." "This part describes well . . ."
Questioning	"I wonder why . . ." "How could . . ." "What does the author mean by . . ."

Text

Comments

MAXIMIZING PROFITS AND EFFICIENCY

During the late 1800s, several factors led to a decline in the quality of working conditions.[1] Machines run by unskilled workers were eliminating the jobs of many skilled craftspeople.[2] These low-paid workers could be replaced easily. Factories began to focus on specialization, or workers repeating a single step again and again. Specialization brought costs down and caused production to rise. But it also made workers tired, bored, and more likely to be injured.[3] Specialization allowed for Henry Ford's idea of a moving assembly line to speed production. Ford's use of the moving assembly line allowed automobiles to be made more quickly and cheaply.[4] Automobiles soon became available to a wider segment of the population than ever before.

In 1909 Frederick W. Taylor, an efficiency engineer, published a popular book called *The Principles of Scientific Management*.[5] He encouraged managers to view workers as interchangeable parts of the production process. In factories, managers influenced by Taylor paid less attention to working conditions. Injuries increased, and as conditions grew worse, workers looked for ways to bring about change.[6]

From *United States History*, The Industrial Age

1 *It sounds like I'm going to read about some bad working conditions and what caused them.*

2 *I already know there were a lot of inventions during this time period. Elimination of jobs must have been one of the effects.*

3 *I wonder why they were more likely to get injured. Maybe if they got bored they stopped paying attention to what they were doing.*

4 *This sounds like how I've seen cars being made in commercials on television.*

5 *What does the author mean by "efficiency engineer?"*

6 *I can imagine that things got pretty bad if people were being treated like machines.*

Text

Comments

JEFFERSON OPPOSES THE BANK

Both Jefferson and Madison believed that Hamilton's plans for the economy gave too much power to the federal government.[1] They also thought the U.S. Constitution did not give Congress the power to create a bank. But Hamilton quoted the elastic clause, which states that Congress can "make all laws which shall be necessary and proper" to govern the nation.[2]

> [1] *I just read about Hamilton's plan for a national bank. I guess Jefferson and Madison didn't like his plan.*

> [2] *"Elastic clause" is a funny term, but I guess it makes sense.*

Hamilton declared that the clause allowed the government to create a national bank. Hamilton believed in loose construction of the Constitution. Loose construction means that the federal government can take reasonable actions that the Constitution does not specifically forbid.[3]

> [3] *This part is difficult. I'd better re-read so I make sure I understand loose construction.*

Jefferson thought that the elastic clause should be used only in special cases.[4] He wrote to President Washington, "The Constitution allows only the means which are 'necessary,' not those which are merely 'convenient.'" Jefferson believed in strict construction of the Constitution.[5] People who favor strict construction think that the federal government should do only what the Constitution specifically says it can do.

> [4] *I wonder what kind of things Jefferson considered special cases.*

> [5] *I can already guess what strict construction is because it sounds like the opposite of loose construction.*

President Washington and Congress agreed with Hamilton.[6] They hoped a bank would offer stability for the U.S. economy. In February 1791 Congress enacted the charter for the Bank of the United States—the country's first national bank. The bank played an important role in making the U.S. economy more stable.

> [6] *If they agreed with Hamilton, they must have set up a national bank. I bet that's what I'm going to read about next.*

From *United States History*, Launching the Nation

Text

Comments

RUSH TO CALIFORNIA

The mass migration to California of miners—and businesspeople who made money off the miners—is known as the gold rush.[1] The migrants who left for California in 1849 were called forty-niners. Their numbers approached a stunning 80,000.

> **1** It sounds like I'm about to read about the California gold rush.

Many more soon followed. Although the dream of finding gold brought people from around the world, three-fourths of those arriving in California came from the United States. To reach California, most people traveled over land, following the California Trail.[2] Others booked passage on ships that sailed all the way around the southern tip of South America.[3] Still others sailed south to Panama, crossed Central America by mule train, and then sailed north to California.[4] By 1854 a full 300,000 people had migrated to California.

> **2** It sounds like they didn't have roads back then. The California Trail must have been a trail across the United States leading to California.

> **3** I think that means they went way out of their way to get there.

> **4** I wonder what the fastest way to get there was.

Upon reaching California, most miners moved into camps in the gold fields.[5] Many others—especially businesspeople—settled in cities. San Francisco, the port nearest the gold fields, had a population of about 200 in 1848. One year later some 25,000 people lived there.[6] By 1860 it was home to some 60,000 people.

> **5** This part reminds me of camp. I wonder if they lived in tents.

> **6** I can just imagine how crowded and busy that city must have been during the gold rush.

The town of Stockton, located on the San Joaquin River on the way to the southern gold fields, boomed. Sacramento, located on the Sacramento River between San Francisco and the northern gold fields, also grew rapidly. When California became the thirty-first state in 1850, Sacramento became its capital.[7]

> **7** I like this part because it kind of explains how California grew.

From *American Anthem*, Expansion Leads to Conflict

Text　　　　　　　　　　　　　　　　　　　　　　**Comments**

CONSERVING FOOD AND OTHER GOODS

Meeting the food needs of the military took top priority in the United States. The planting of victory gardens was one way in which Americans filled these needs.[1]

1　*I don't really remember what victory gardens were. I should go back and review.*

Victory gardens alone did not solve all the nation's food needs. Some foods could not be produced in home gardens, and there was simply not enough of certain products to go around.[2] As a result, the United States began rationing food shortly after the nation entered the war.[3] Rationing means limiting the amount of a certain product each individual can get.

2　*I can imagine that it might be hard for most people to raise cows for meat and milk in a home garden.*

3　*I don't know what rationing is. I'd better keep reading to see if I can figure it out.*

During the war, the government rationed products such as coffee, butter, sugar, and meat.[4] Each member of the family received a ration book, which entitled that person to a certain amount of certain foods. Most people willingly accepted the system. Penalties for breaking the rationing rules could be severe.[5]

4　*I wonder if that means people went hungry.*

5　*This part makes it sound like rationing was like a law.*

The war effort also meant shortages of other materials, such as metal, glass, rubber, and gasoline. Gasoline was rationed.[6] Americans helped meet the demand for other materials by holding scrap drives, in which citizens collected waste material of all sorts that might be used in the war efforts. Empty tin cans, bits of rubber and glass—anything that could be useful was salvaged.[7] Even women's silk and nylon stockings were recycled to make parachutes.[8]

6　*I think this means that people probably didn't drive cars as much during the war.*

7　*This reminds me of the recycling that my city does.*

8　*That's funny to think of a parachute made out of stockings.*

Scrap drives provided a way for young Americans to help with the war effort. Scouts and other youth organizations helped lead the way in this important national effort.

From *American Anthem*, The United States in World War II

Text

SCIENCE AND RELIGION

The Roman Catholic Church was a powerful force in Europe during the time of the Scientific Revolution. The birth and growth of science led to conflicts between scientists and the Church.[1]

There were two related parts to the conflict between science and the Church. The first was that the new science was putting forth ideas that contradicted Church teachings. For example, Copernicus's idea that the earth orbited the sun contradicted the Church teaching that the earth was at the center of the universe.[2]

A second part of the conflict was related to the first. When people contradicted the Church's teachings, they weakened the Church.[3] Church officials were afraid that questioning even one Church teaching might lead to more and more questions about the Church. People might even start to doubt key elements of the faith. Church officials feared this would undermine the Church's influence.[4]

The conflict between science and the Church was illustrated by a trial. Galileo published a book that supported the view that the planets orbit the sun. For this, he was put on trial by the Inquisition, a Church court that investigated people who questioned Church authority.[5]

Catholic officials insisted that Galileo publicly reject his findings and accept Catholic teachings that the earth was the center of the universe and did not move. Under threat of torture, Galileo agreed.[6] Still, legend has it that as Galileo left his trial, he muttered, "And yet it does move."[7]

From *World History,* The Scientific Revolution

1 *I wonder what the conflicts were. That must be what I'm going to learn about next.*

2 *That reminds me of something I learned in science. I've seen pictures of the earth and other planets orbiting the sun.*

3 *How could they do that? I'd better read to find out.*

4 *I don't know what "undermine" means. But I guess it means something like "hurt" because Church officials feared it.*

5 *Why did the Church have a court? The Church was pretty powerful back then, so I guess they could pretty much do what they wanted.*

6 *I can see that Galileo must have been scared. I wonder what I would have done if I had been threatened.*

7 *I bet that means Galileo didn't really believe those Church teachings. It sounds like he just agreed so he could go free.*

Text

ARISTOCRATS AND TYRANTS RULE

Greece is the birthplace of democracy, a type of government in which people rule themselves.[1] The word democracy comes from Greek words meaning "rule of the people." But Greek city-states didn't start as democracies, and not all became democratic.[2]

Even Athens, the city where democracy was born, began with a different kind of government. In early Athens, kings ruled the city-state. Later, a group of rich landowners, or aristocrats, took power. A government in which only a few people have power is called an oligarchy.[3]

The aristocrats dominated Athenian society. As the richest men in town, they ran the city's economy. They also served as its generals and judges. Common people had little say in the government.[4]

In the 600s BC a group of rebels tried to overthrow the aristocrats. They failed. Possibly as a result of their attempt, however, a man named Draco created a new set of laws for Athens. These laws were very harsh.[5] For example, Draco's laws made minor crimes such as loitering punishable by death.[6]

The people of Athens thought Draco's laws were too strict. In the 590s BC a man named Solon created a set of laws that were much less harsh and gave more rights to nonaristocrats. Under Solon's laws, all free men living in Athens became citizens, people who had the right to participate in government.[7] But his efforts were not enough for Athenians. They were ready to end the rule of the aristocracy.

From *World History*, Ancient Greece

1 *I already know what democracy is. It's the kind of government we have in the United States.*

2 *It sounds like this next part is going to be about some Greek city-state that wasn't a democracy.*

3 *This is confusing. So, an oligarchy is a government ruled by a few rich people.*

4 *I can see how common people might not be happy with Athenian society.*

5 *I bet Draco's laws were to keep people from trying to rebel.*

6 *What does loitering mean? It must not be all that bad if it's just a minor crime.*

7 *This sounds like the beginnings of democracy, because people participate in their government in a democracy.*

Reading Social Studies

Text

Comments

GHANA BUILDS AN EMPIRE

By 800 Ghana was firmly in control of West Africa's trade routes. Nearly all trade between northern and southern Africa passed through Ghana. Ghana's army kept the trade routes safe. Trade increased, and so did Ghana's wealth.[1]

1 *It sounds like I'm going to read about Ghana's wealth.*

With so many traders passing through their lands, Ghana's rulers looked for ways to profit from their dealings. One way was to force every trader who entered Ghana to pay a special tax on the goods he carried. Then each trader had to pay another tax on the goods he took with him when he left. The people of Ghana also had to pay taxes.[2] In addition, Ghana forced small neighboring tribes to pay tribute.[3]

2 *This sounds like the United States. People have to pay taxes here, too.*

3 *I don't know what tribute means. Maybe it's another kind of tax.*

Ghana's gold mines brought even more income into the royal treasury. Some gold was carried by traders to lands as far away as England.[4] But not all of Ghana's gold was traded. Ghana's kings also kept huge stores of the precious metal for themselves.

4 *I wonder how they got all the way to England back then.*

The rulers of Ghana banned everyone else in Ghana from owning gold nuggets. Common people could only own gold dust, which they used as money.[5] This ensured that the king was richer than his subjects.

5 *I can just picture people trying to use gold dust as money. It must have been hard to keep track of.*

Part of Ghana's wealth went to support its powerful army.[6] Ghana's kings used this army to conquer many neighboring areas. To keep order in their large empire, Ghana's kings allowed conquered rulers to retain much of their power.[7] These local rulers acted as governors of their territories, answering only to the king.

6 *I already know they needed the army to protect trade routes.*

7 *I wonder how this helped Ghana's kings keep power.*

From *World History*, Early African Civilizations

Reading Social Studies

Text

Comments

THE MONGOL EMPIRE

Among the nomadic people who attacked the Chinese were the Mongols.[1] For centuries, the Mongols had lived as separate tribes in the vast plains north of China. Then in 1206, a powerful leader, or khan, united them. His name was Temüjin. When he became leader, though, he was given a new title: "Universal Ruler," or Genghis Khan.[2]

Genghis Khan organized the Mongols into a powerful army and led them on bloody expeditions of conquest. The brutality of the Mongol attacks terrorized people throughout much of Asia and Eastern Europe. Genghis Khan and his army killed all of the men, women, and children in countless cities and villages.[3] Within 20 years, he ruled a large part of Asia.

Genghis Khan then turned his attention to China. He first led his armies into northern China in 1211. They fought their way south, wrecking whole towns and ruining farmland.[4] By the time of Genghis Khan's death in 1227, all of northern China was under Mongol control.

The Mongol conquests did not end with Genghis Khan's death, though. His sons and grandsons continued to raid lands all over Asia and Eastern Europe . . .[5]

In 1260 Genghis Khan's granson Kublai Khan became ruler of the Mongol Empire. He completed the conquest of China and in 1279 declared himself emperor of China. This began the Yuan dynasty, a period that some people also call the Mongol Ascendancy.[6] For the first time in its long history, foreigners ruled all of China.

From *World History*, China

1 *I think this is going to be about some people called the Mongols attacking China.*

2 *That title makes him sound pretty important. I bet he's going to have a major impact on history.*

3 *I can imagine how bloody those attacks must have been. I wonder why he killed so many people.*

4 *This reminds me of how he fought in other parts of Asia and Eastern Europe.*

5 *I wonder if their raids were as violent and destructive as Genghis Khan's.*

6 *I don't know what Ascendancy means. It must have something to do with the Mongols coming to power.*

Reading Social Studies

Text

CUBA

Cuba is the largest and most populous country in the Caribbean. It is located just 92 miles (148 km) south of Florida. Havana, the capital, is the country's largest and most important city.

Cuba has been run by a Communist government since Fidel Castro came to power in 1959.[1] At that time, the government took over banks, large sugarcane plantations, and other businesses.[2] Many of these businesses were owned by U.S. companies. Because of the takeovers, the U.S. government banned trade with Cuba and restricted travel there by U.S. citizens.

Today the government still controls the economy. Most of Cuba's farms are organized as cooperatives or government-owned plantations. A cooperative is an organization owned by its members and operated for their mutual benefit.[3]

Besides controlling the economy, Cuba's government also controls all the newspapers, television, and radio stations.[4] While many Cubans support Castro and his policies, others oppose them.[5] Some people who oppose Castro have become refugees in the United States. Many Cuban refugees have become U.S. citizens.

From *The Americas*, Central America and the Caribbean

1 *I've read about communism before. I think it's when the government controls the economy.*

2 *I wonder why the government did that. I imagine that it would make a lot of people mad.*

3 *I'm not sure I understand what that means. Maybe I should re-read to see if I can picture it better.*

4 *I don't think I would like it very much if the government controlled what I could watch on television.*

5 *Next I'm probably going to read about people who either support or oppose Castro's policies.*

Text

Comments

WIND, WATER, AND STORMS

If you watch weather reports, you will hear about storms moving across the United States.[1] Tracking storms is important to us because the United States has so many of them. As you will see, some areas of the world have more storms than others do.

Most storms occur when two air masses collide.[2] An air mass is a large body of air. The place where two air masses of different temperatures or moisture content meet is a front.[3] Air masses frequently collide in regions like the United States, where the westerlies meet the polar easterlies.[4]

Fronts can produce rain or snow as well as severe weather such as thunderstorms and icy blizzards. Thunderstorms produce rain, lightning, and thunder. In the United states, they are most common in spring and summer.[5] Blizzards produce strong winds and large amounts of snow and are most common during winter.

Thunderstorms and blizzards can also produce tornadoes, another type of severe storm. A tornado is a small, rapidly twisting funnel of air that touches the ground. Tornadoes usually affect a limited area and last only a few minutes. However, they can be highly destructive, uprooting trees and tossing large vehicles through the air.[6] Tornadoes can be extremely deadly as well . . .

The largest and most destructive storms, however, are hurricanes. These large, rotating storms form over tropical waters in the Atlantic Ocean, usually from late sumer to fall. Did you know that hurricanes and typhoons are the same? Typhoons are just hurricanes that form in the Pacific Ocean.[7]

From *Introduction to Geography*, Climate, Environment, and Resources

1 *I know about this because I've seen weather reports on the news.*

2 *I don't get what the author means by an "air mass." I'd better keep reading.*

3 *This reminds me of what I've heard on weather reports.*

4 *I don't remember what westerlies and easterlies are. I'd better go back and review.*

5 *This sounds like weather we have at home sometimes.*

6 *I can just picture a car flying through the air. That would be really scary.*

7 *I wonder why they have different names for the same type of storm.*

Reading Social Studies

Text

Comments

ECONOMY

The level of economic development in the Indian Perimeter is generally low. The countries depend heavily on agriculture.[1] Most have tried to build new industries. However, these efforts have been slowed by a lack of natural resources.[2] Despite these similarities, there is quite a range between the richest and poorest countries of the region. For example, Nepal and Bhutan are among the poorest countries in the world. Yet Pakistan, while still a poor country, has experienced growth in GDP since independence.[3]

Pakistan has used its significant mineral resources to help develop its manufacturing industries. However, nearly half the labor force still works in agriculture. Although Pakistan's economy has grown, so has its population. This population growth strains the country's ability to provide basic services to its people.

Bangladesh is overwhelmingly agricultural.[4] More than half of the people work in farming. Jute, rice, and tea are the most important crops.[5] Farming depends on the monsoon.[6] Variations in the timing and intensity of the monsoon rains make the difference between a good harvest or a poor one.[7] In recent times people have built a number of irrigation projects to control floods and conserve water for the dry months. These projects, the increased use of fertilizers, and new crops have increased farm output.

From *World Geography Today*, The Indian Perimeter

1 *I have read about many other countries that depend on agriculture. They are mostly poor also.*

2 *I already know you need natural resources like minerals to have industry.*

3 *I think this means that Pakistan is not as poor as those other countries.*

4 *I bet I'm going to read about agriculture in Bangladesh now.*

5 *I wonder what jute is.*

6 *I don't remember what a monsoon is. I'd better keep reading.*

7 *From this part I can see that crops must need just the right amount of rain.*

Reading Social Studies

Text

Comments

NATURAL INCREASE

Geographers are interested in the rate of natural population growth, or natural increase.[1] This rate is based just on births and deaths—it does not take migration into account.[2] You can find the rate by subtracting the death rate from the birthrate. This final number is expressed as a percentage. In the United States, the rate of natural increase is about 0.6 percent each year.[3]

The rate of natural increase varies greatly in countries around the world. The highest rates are found in countries in Africa and Southwest Asia. Rates there are sometimes 3 percent or higher.[4] The number of people living in those places is rising rapidly. Most countries in Central and South America and in Southeast Asia have more moderate rates of natural increase. The rates for these areas are somewhere between 1 and 3 percent. The lowest rates—less than 1 percent—are found in most European and North American countries. Australia, New Zealand, and Japan also have such low rates. Some countries, such as Italy and Russia, actually have negative growth rates.[5] The number of people living in these countries is decreasing.

These percentages—1, 2, and 3—may sound small. However, they can add up to large population increases in a short period of time. For example, suppose the number of people living in a country grows at a rate of 3 percent. That country's population will double in only about 23 years![6] Geographers call the number of years needed to double a country's population its doubling time.[7]

From *World Geography Today*, Human Geography

1 *It sounds like I'm going to read about population growth now.*

2 *I know migration changes the population of a country, so natural increase must not measure total population growth.*

3 *This part is confusing. I'd better read it again slowly and think about it.*

4 *That's funny. Three percent doesn't seem very high to me.*

5 *I wonder why some countries have negative growth rates.*

6 *I can picture all the building that would have to take place to give all those people homes.*

7 *I like that. Doubling time is a good name for it.*

Reading Social Studies

Text

Comments

CONGRESS AND THE CONSTITUTION

Congress often applies the Constitution to a particular issue in society.[1] It does this by interpreting whether some passage, or clause, in the Constitution gives Congress the authority to pass a particular law.

> **1** It sounds like I'm about to read about the Constitution and society.

For example, the Constitution says nothing about whether all workers should earn a minimum wage.[2] However, the Constitution does give Congress the power to control trade among the states. Goods made by workers usually travel from one state to another. So Congress decided that the Constitution gives it the power to pass laws affecting working conditions nationwide, including wage rates.[3] It then wrote laws establishing a minimum wage.

> **2** I already know that there is a law that people have to make at least the minimum wage.

> **3** This part about trade between the states is confusing. I'd better re-read it to see if I can figure out the connection to the minimum wage.

The Supreme Court has the power to decide if Congress has interpreted the Constitution correctly. The Court's interpretation is final. If the Supreme Court rules that a law is unconstitutional, the law is dead. If the Court upholds the law, it remains in effect.[4]

> **4** This part describes well the effect the Supreme Court can have on a law.

If the Supreme Court declares an act of Congress unconstitutional, Congress may rewrite the law. If Congress overcomes the Court's objections, the new law will stand.[5]

> **5** What does the author mean by "stand?" It must mean the law is okay.

For example, Congress may not pass bills of attainder (laws which punish a person without a jury trial) or ex post facto laws (which make an act a crime after the act has been committed).[6] Congress also may not suspend the writ of habeas corpus (a court order requiring the government to bring a prisoner to court and explain why he or she is being held).

> **6** I already know Congress can't pass laws that go against the Constitution. These laws must already be in the Constitution.

From *Civics in Practice*, The United States Constitution

Reading Social Studies

Text

Comments

THE HOUSE OF REPRESENTATIVES

According to the Constitution, the number of representatives each state can elect to the House is based on the state's population.[1] Each state is entitled to at least one representative. Washington, D.C., Guam, American Samoa, and the Virgin Islands each have one nonvoting delegate in the House.[2]

Today there are 435 members in the House. Why 435 members? In 1789, when the first Congress met, the Constitution allowed for 65 representatives in the House. Each state elected one representative for every 30,000 people in the state. However, as new states joined the Union and the population increased, membership in the House kept growing. Eventually, Congress had to limit the size of the House to 435 members.[3]

Every 10 years, after the census is taken, Congress determines how the seats in the House are to be apportioned, or distributed.[4] If a state's population decreases, the number of its representatives may be reduced.[5] States whose populations grow may be entitled to more representatives.

Voters elect their representative according to the congressional district in which they live.[6] Each state's legislature is responsible for dividing the state into as many congressional districts as it has members in the House of Representatives. District boundaries must be drawn so that each district is almost equal in population.

From *Civics in Practice*, The Legislative Branch

1 *I think this means that big states probably have more representatives than small states.*

2 *I wonder why these representatives aren't allowed to vote.*

3 *I can see that the House would have gotten way too big if it had kept growing with the population.*

4 *I've heard about the census. That's when they count the people in the country.*

5 *Next it's probably going to tell me about states whose populations have increased.*

6 *I don't know what a congressional district is. Maybe if I keep reading I'll figure it out.*

Text

Comments

THE VICE PRESIDENCY

For much of the country's history, a vice president had very little to do. What are the responsibilities of the modern vice president?[1] One very important responsibility is to serve as president if the president dies, leaves office, or is unable to fulfill his or her duties.[2] Eight presidents have died while in office and one president resigned. In each case, the vice president was sworn in as president. The vice president also serves a four-year term and must meet the same constitutional qualifications as the president.[3] The vice president receives a salary of $186,300 a year, plus a $10,000 taxable expense allowance.[4]

The vice president has only one other job defined in the Constitution—to preside over the Senate. However, the vice president is not a member of the Senate. He or she cannot take part in Senate debates and may vote only in the case of a tie.[5]

In recent years, presidents have given their vice presidents more responsibilities than those described by the Constitution. Presidents often send their vice presidents to represent the United States overseas. Vice presidents usually work closely with the president in order to be fully informed on the issues. For example, Vice President Dick Cheney has an important role on President Bush's team, becoming involved in developing policy and in gathering support for the president's programs.[6]

From *Civics in Practice*, The Executive Branch

1 *It sounds like I'm going to learn about the responsibilities of the vice president.*

2 *I wonder why a president wouldn't be able to fulfill his or her duties.*

3 *I already know about the qualifications for the president because I read about them earlier.*

4 *I don't know what the author means by a taxable expense allowance. It sounds like it's just more money.*

5 *It doesn't seem like the vice president has many official jobs.*

6 *This reminds me of what I've seen in the newspaper and on the news.*

Text

Comments

A NATION OF LAWS

There are two basic categories of laws, criminal law and civil law.[1] When people talk about "breaking the law," they are usually referring to a crime.[2] A crime is any behavior that is illegal because society, through its government, considers the behavior harmful to society. Criminal law refers to the group of laws that define what acts are crimes. Criminal law also describes how a person accused of a crime should be tried in court and how crimes should be punished.[3]

Criminal laws are intended to protect society as a whole. For example, laws against assault, murder, and rape help protect you and other people from being harmed. Laws against stealing help protect your property and other people's property as well. You might think that a crime against another person does not affect you, but that is not true.[4] If someone who breaks into your neighbor's house and steals something is not caught and punished, the criminal may steal again. The criminal might even break into your house next. And if criminals are not caught and punished, people may begin to think that it is okay to steal.[5]

The other basic category of laws is civil law. Civil law is the group of laws that refer to disputes between people. If you have a dispute with someone and you cannot solve it privately, you may go to court to settle the matter. In court, the judge and maybe a jury will listen to the facts of the case. The judge will then apply the civil law and make a decision. Civil laws are used to settle a wide range of personal issues, such as contract disputes, divorce proceedings, and property boundaries.[6]

From *Civics in Practice*, The Judicial Branch

1 *It sounds like I'm going to learn about the kinds of laws in this country.*

2 *I know this is right because I've heard people talk about breaking the law.*

3 *Those are some pretty confusing definitions. I'd better re-read this part slowly.*

4 *How does a crime against another person affect me?*

5 *I can see how punishments would keep people from doing bad things.*

6 *This part explains well what kinds of things are covered under civil law.*

How to Use Graphic Organizers

Graphic organizers are a valuable tool for teaching and studying social studies because they provide many different ways to organize information. Each graphic organizer in this book can be used with any social studies subject. The chart below shows the graphic organizers included in this book. For each graphic organizer, there is a suggestion about topics for which that graphic organizer is best suited.

Type of Graphic Organizer	Suggested Uses
Web Diagram	• Identifying details about historical figures or events, etc. • Identifying qualities of natural formations, etc. • Identifying cultural or physical features of a country, etc.
Cause and Effect Diagram	• Explaining the cause and effect of a historical event, such as World War 1 • Analyzing the cause of a geographic occurrence, such as land erosion • Explaining the cause and effect of an economic situation, such as a recession
Cause and Effect Chain	• Explaining the effects of a historical event, such as an assassination • Explaining the effects of a presidential election • Analyzing the effects of a geographic occurrence, such as erosion
Sequence Chain	• Studying a sequence of historical events • Understanding a political process, such as steps in a bill becoming a law • Analyzing a geographic process, such as the evaporation of water
Comparison-Contrast Chart	• Comparing/contrasting causes and effects of two battles or wars • Comparing/contrasting two economic or political systems • Comparing/contrasting resources in different locations

Type of Graphic Organizer	Suggested Uses
Venn Diagram	• Comparing/contrasting historical figures, time periods, etc. • Comparing/contrasting countries, regions, cities, etc. • Analyzing two trends, systems, laws, etc.
Main Idea and Details Chart	• Identifying main ideas and details about historical figures, time periods, etc. • Forming main ideas and details about countries, regions, cities, etc. • Understanding main ideas and details about economic conditions, governmental structures, etc.
Determining Main Idea Chart	• Studying details about a topic, such as inflation or capitalism, to arrive at a main idea • Using details about a historical event or a culture to arrive at a main idea • Examining details about a topic, such as migration or population, to arrive at a main idea
KWL Chart	• Reading about historical figures, time periods, etc. • Studying countries, regions, cities, etc. • Researching political issues, legal topics, etc.
Positive-Negative Chart	• Evaluating positive and negative effects of a change in power • Judging good and bad consequences of changing the environment • Evaluating pros and cons of changing requirements for citizenship
Evaluation Pyramid	• Evaluating the importance of reasons for the rise and fall of an empire • Ranking most important U.S. presidents • Judging the most important factors in a country's economy
Conclusions Chart	• Drawing conclusions about the effects of agricultural practices • Determining the effectiveness of a leader • Drawing conclusions about the effect of a law

Web Diagram

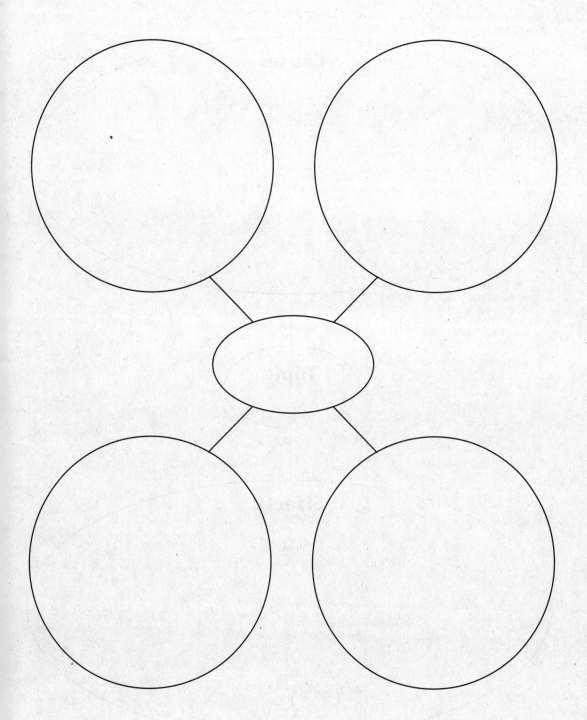

Cause and Effect Diagram

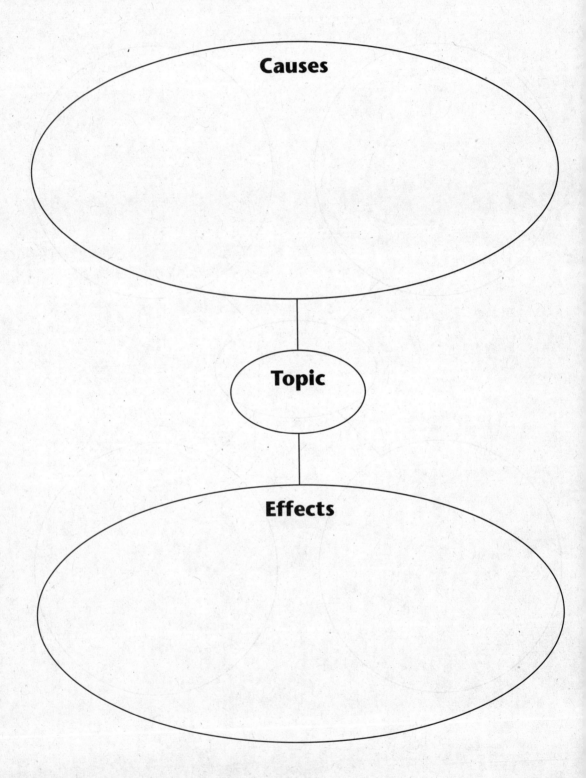

Cause and Effect Chain

Graphic Organizers

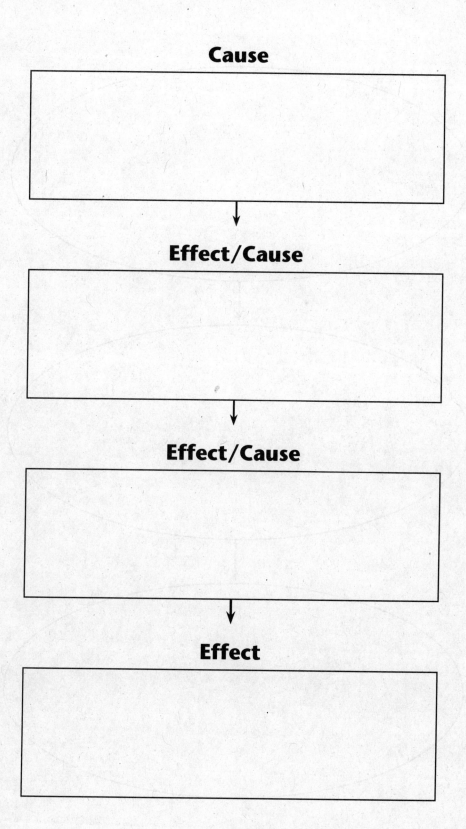

Cause

Effect/Cause

Effect/Cause

Effect

Sequence Chain   Graphic Organizers

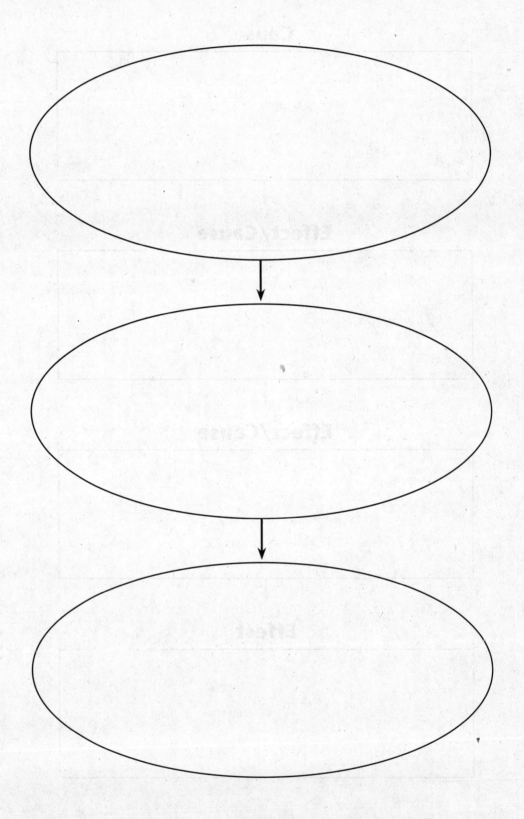

Comparison-Contrast Chart

Graphic Organizers

	(Subject 1)	(Subject 2)
(Point A)		
(Point B)		
(Point C)		
(Point D)		

Venn Diagram   Graphic Organizers

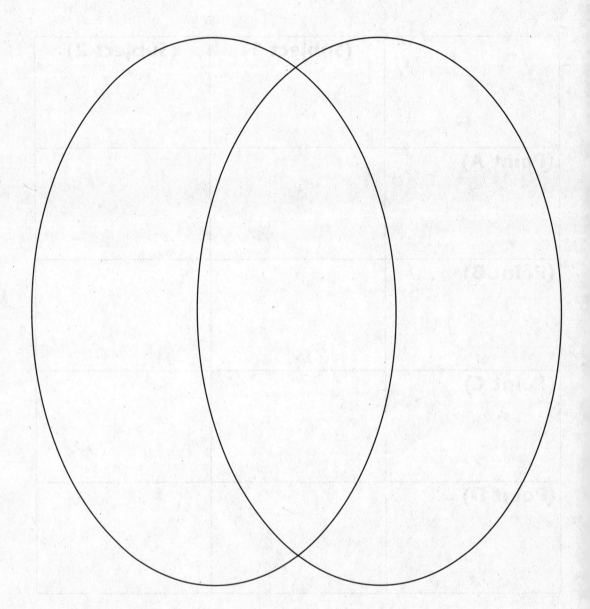

Main Idea and Details Chart

Main Idea

↓

Supporting Detail 1
Supporting Detail 2
Supporting Detail 3

Determining Main Idea Chart

Topic	
Important Details	
Main Idea	

Topic	
Important Details	
Main Idea	

Reading Social Studies

Name _____ Class _____ Date _____

KWL Chart   Graphic Organizers

Topic: _____

K What I *Know*	W What I *Want* To Learn	L What I Have *Learned*

Reading Social Studies

Positive-Negative Chart

Positive

Negative

94

Evaluation Pyramid

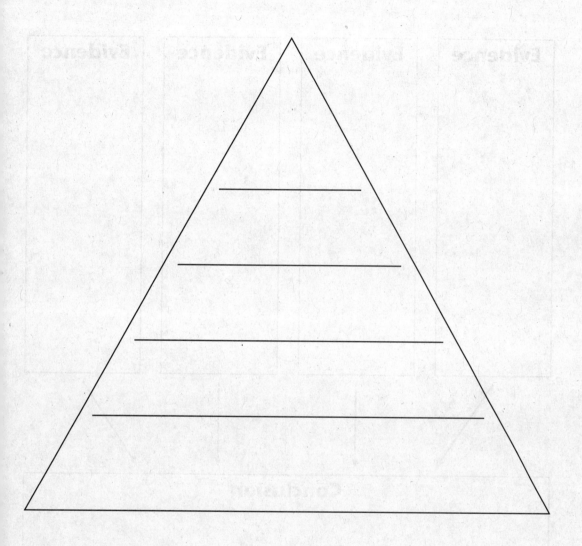

Conclusions Chart

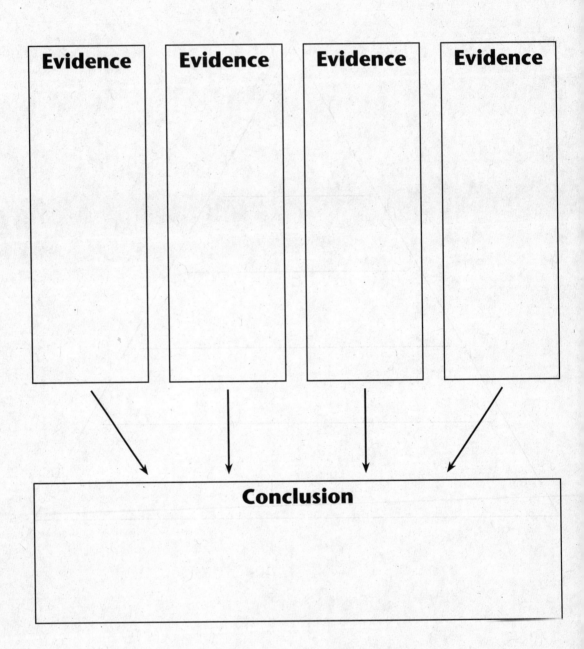

Evidence | **Evidence** | **Evidence** | **Evidence**

Conclusion

Reading Social Studies

Reading Skills

SETTING A PURPOSE

Reading American History

Answers will vary. Sample responses:

Heading   Devastation in the Dust Bowl

Question   What is the Dust Bowl? What happened there that was so bad?

Purpose   I'll read to find out more about the Dust Bowl and the bad things that happened there during the Depression.

Reading World History

Answers will vary. Sample responses:

Feature   Main idea: Greeks created myths to explain the world.

Question   I wonder what myths they created and what they tried to explain about the world.

Purpose   I'll read to discover what kinds of myths they created and what kinds of things they wanted to explain.

Reading Geography

Answers will vary. Sample responses:

Feature   Main Idea: Rwanda and Burundi are densely populated rural countries with a history of ethnic conflict.

Question   How has the high population and ethnic conflict affected these countries?

Purpose   I'll read to learn what caused ethnic conflict and how it has affected Rwanda and Burundi.

Reading Civics

Answers will vary. Sample responses:

Heading   Legislative Leader

Question   I know about the legislature. What does the president have to do with it?

Purpose   I'll read to find out more about how the president leads and influences the legislature.

MAKING PREDICTIONS

Reading American History

Answers will vary. Sample responses:

What I know   Some teens express rebellion by wearing different clothes and hairstyles and listening to different music than adults.

New information   The 1960s was a time of rebellion.

Prediction   Teens and young adults found ways to express rebellion in the 1960s through music, dress, and lifestyles.

Reading World History

Answers will vary. Sample responses:

What I know   Artists paint pictures of religious scenes, make religious symbols, and do sculptures.

New information   The church was a big influence on art in the Middle Ages.

Prediction   There were many religious paintings, sculptures, and symbols, in addition to cathedrals, created during the Middle Ages.

Reading Geography

Answers will vary. Sample responses:

What I know   Large populations lead to crowded cities, not enough food, and poor housing.

New information   Kenya is having a population explosion.

Prediction   Kenya is facing crowded cities, famine, and poor housing.

Reading Civics

Answers will vary. Sample responses:

What I know   There are laws about downloading music from the Internet.

New information   Congress makes laws that affect our lives.

Prediction   Congress has the authority to make laws about downloading music from the Internet.

IDENTIFYING MAIN IDEAS AND DETAILS

Reading American History

Main idea   Cars helped other industries.

Main details   automobile materials; repair shops and gas stations; motels and restaurants

Reading World History

Main idea   Rome was a dangerous place.

Main details   war; political riots; more people moving to the city

Reading Geography

Main idea   Ireland and Great Britain have similar cultures.

Main details   social life; sports; English language

Reading Civics

Main idea   The Speaker is the most powerful member of the House of Representatives.

Main details   member of majority party; calls on representatives to speak; influences order of business

SUMMARIZING

Reading American History

Summary of Paragraph 2   Twelve Nazis were sentenced to die and several others got long jail sentences.

Summary of Paragraph 3   Other countries also tried and convicted Nazis in response to the Holocaust.

Combined Summary   The International Military Tribunal and other trials after World War II tried and convicted Nazis who were responsible for the Holocaust.

Reading World History

Summary of Paragraph 2   Some young boys discovered the Dead Sea Scrolls in a cave in 1947.

Summary of Paragraph 3   Scholars found more scrolls in the next few decades.

Summary of Paragraph 4   The scrolls were writings from the Hebrew Bible that were written between 100 BC and AD 50.

Combined Summary   The Dead Sea Scrolls are part of the Hebrew Bible and help to explain ancient Jewish beliefs. They were written between 100 BC and AD 50, but weren't discovered until 1947.

Reading Geography

Summary of Paragraph 2   Moscow has many economic advantages.

Summary of Paragraph 3   A large transportation network allows millions of Russians to live and work in Moscow.

Combined Summary   Million of Russians live and work in their capital city of Moscow, which is also the country's economic and religious center.

Reading Civics

Summary of Paragraph 2   The mass media and communications technology make this the propaganda age.

Summary of Paragraph 3   Advertisers and political candidates use propaganda to influence public opinion.

Combined Summary   Propaganda is used so often by advertisers and political candidates to influence public opinion that today is known as the propaganda age.

MAKING INFERENCES

Reading American History

Answers will vary. Sample responses:

Information "inside the text"   At first, soldiers did not have uniforms. They did not know how to fight. Some did not have weapons or they had poor quality weapons.

Information "outside the text"   It would be confusing if soldiers didn't have uniforms. Soldiers usually go through training before going to battle. Poor quality weapons probably were not very accurate.

Inference   The first battles of the Civil War were probably confusing and disorganized for both sides.

Reading World History

Answers will vary. Sample responses:

Information "inside the text" Aryans lived in small communities based on family ties. Rajas from different villages were often engaged in war.

Information "outside the text" It takes a lot of organization to build big cities like the Harappans did. War takes time and resources from other activities.

Inference The Aryans probably didn't build big cities because rulers spent time at war instead of joining together and planning cities.

Reading Geography
Answers will vary. Sample responses:

Information "inside the text" The weather is dry in the winter. The weather is rainy in the summer. It is warm in the winter and the summer.

Information "outside the text" People like to get away from cold weather. People don't enjoy rainy weather on vacations.

Inference The busiest season for toursim for Central America and the Caribbean is probably the winter.

Reading Civics
Answers will vary. Sample responses:

Information "inside the text" Americans have free speech. Some governments punish people if they criticize the government.

Information "outside the text" People criticize when they don't like someone or something. If people keep criticizing, more people will notice what is wrong. Criticism sometimes lead to changes.

Inference Some governments punish people who criticize because they don't want people to demand changes.

SEQUENCING
Reading American History
First Allies invade Sicily in July 1943.
Next Italians turn against Mussolini.
Next The Allies take Sicily a few weeks later.
Last The Allies make progress through Italy despite German resistance.

Reading World History
First New leaders rose to power in the 1500s.
Next Oda Nobunaga defeated his opponents.
Next Tokugawa became shogun in 1603.
Last The Tokugawa shogunate lasted until 1868.

Reading Geography
First The sun heats water on Earth's surface.
Next Water vapor rises into the air.
Next Water vapor turns to liquid droplets and falls to Earth as precipitation.
Last Water is absorbed by soil or collects in streams, rivers, and oceans.

Reading Civics
First Lawyers present arguments to the Court.
Next Justices read and think about arguments.
Next Justices vote on case in a private meeting.
Last Justices explain the opinion of the court.

IDENTIFYING CAUSE AND EFFECT
Reading American History
Cause land boom ended
Cause The Big Blow hurricane
Effect economic depression in Florida

Reading World History
Cause Napoleon takes over
Effect Code of Napoleon
Effect Bank of France

Reading World Geography
Cause Aswan High Dam built on Nile
Effect hydroelectric power
Effect/Cause water to irrigate farms
Effect new lands for farmers

Reading Civics

Cause   Americans trusted militias to defend communities, not armies.

Cause   Militias defended against attacks from Indians.

Effect   creation of the Second Amendment

COMPARING AND CONTRASTING

Reading American History

Similar   president, favored business regulation, opposed socialism, antitrust lawsuits

Different   Roosevelt—claimed more power, sought strict regulation of big business; Taft—moved cautiously toward reform and regulation

Reading World History

Similar   democratic, citizens participate

Different   Ancient Greece—direct democracy, each person's decision directly affects vote, citizens gathered to discuss issues and vote; United States—too big for direct democracy, impossible for all citizens to gather in one place

Reading World Geography

Similar   important rivers, have cities and industrial areas along banks, barges carry goods, flow through Germany, pollution is a problem

Different   Rhine—begins in Swiss Alps, empties into North Sea; Danube—begins in Germany, flows through nine countries, empties into Black Sea

Reading Civics

Similar   mayor and city council both have power

Different   weak-mayor plan—council holds most power, council appoints department heads, more conflict between council and mayor; strong-mayor plan—mayor holds most power, mayor appoints city officials, more efficient

IDENTIFYING PROBLEMS AND SOLUTIONS

Reading American History

Problem   high inflation and unemployment

Solution   freeze in wages and prices

Outcome   temporarily lowered inflation, but effect did not last

Reading World History

Problem   People didn't know Rome's laws.

Solution   Laws were written down and posted in Forum.

Outcome   Romans saw laws as symbols of rights as citizens.

Reading Geography

Problem   Poor infrastructure and economy.

Solution   Replacing outdated factories, encouraging tourism.

Outcome   Cities have grown as industrial centers and are popular with tourists.

Reading Civics

Problem   Delegates couldn't agree on type of representation.

Solution   Great Compromise created Senate and House.

Outcome   both sides happy, still works today

DRAWING CONCLUSIONS

Reading American History

Answers will vary. Sample responses:

Information from the text   He wanted to reduce tensions between religious groups. He presented a bill to allow religious freedoms. The bill only applied to Christians.

Conclusion   Lord Baltimore thought that Christians should be allowed to worship as they pleased.

Reading World History

Answers will vary. Sample responses:

Information from the text   Wudi's government was based on Confucianism. Confucius taught that people should respect their father and leaders. Government officials thought that if people obeyed the father, then they would obey the emperor.

Conclusion The ancient Chinese viewed Wudi as a father of the country, someone to be respected and obeyed.

Reading Geography

Answers will vary. Sample responses:

Information from the text Water is used to irrigate cotton fields. Little water flows into the Aral Sea. Countries have built dams on the rivers for hydroelectricity.

Conclusion People in Uzbekistan and Turkmenistan may have different views over whether the limited river water should be used mostly for irrigation or for hydroelectricity.

Reading Civics

Answers will vary. Sample responses:

Information from the text Tariffs raise prices on imported goods. Tariffs protect American industry from competition. Tariffs provide money for the government.

Conclusion People would be able to buy more imported goods, but American industry might suffer and the government would collect less money.

MAKING GENERALIZATIONS

Reading American History

Answers will vary. Sample responses:

From the text U.S. had goal of containment. U.S. gave money to Greece and Turkey. Providing aid became Truman Doctrine.

Generalization The U.S. gave money to countries to help them stay free from Soviet influence and communism.

Reading World History

Answers will vary. Sample responses:

From the text Napoleon removed royalists in 48 hours. He had dazzling victories over Italian and Austrian troops. He stopped a French rebellion. He became general when he was only 26.

Generalization Napoleon was a very talented and successful military leader.

Reading Geography

Answers will vary. Sample responses:

From the text Mexico City is the world's second-largest city. It has job and educational opportunities. It is polluted. It has a mix of wealth and poverty.

Generalization Mexico City is a huge city with many opportunities and challenges.

Reading Civics

Answers will vary. Sample responses:

From the text Congress has passed acts to limit campaign contributions. Limits are enforced.

Generalization Spending limits keep people from giving unlimitied amounts of money to political campaigns.

Think-Alouds

READING AMERICAN HISTORY

Model 1
1. Predicting what happens next
2. Connecting
3. Identifying and fixing problems in understanding
4. Making comparisons
5. Questioning
6. Picturing the text

Model 2
1. Connecting
2. Making comments
3. Identifying and fixing problems in understanding
4. Questioning
5. Making comparisons
6. Predicting what happens next

Model 3
1. Predicting what happens next
2. Connecting
3. Making comments
4. Questioning
5. Making comparisons

Answer Key

6. Picturing the text
7. Making comments

Model 4

1. Identifying and fixing problems in understanding
2. Picturing the text
3. Identifying and fixing problems in understanding
4. Questioning
5. Making comparisons
6. Making comments
7. Connecting
8. Making comments

READING WORLD HISTORY

Model 1

1. Predicting what happens next
2. Connecting
3. Questioning
4. Identifying and fixing problems in understanding
5. Connecting
6. Picturing the text, Making comparisons
7. Making comments

Model 2

1. Making comparisons
2. Predicting what happens next
3. Identifying and fixing problems in understanding
4. Making comments
5. Making comments
6. Questioning
7. Connecting

Model 3

1. Predicting what happens next
2. Making comparisons
3. Identifying and fixing problems in understanding
4. Questioning
5. Picturing the text
6. Connecting
7. Questioning

Model 4

1. Predicting what happens next
2. Making comments
3. Picturing the text, Questioning
4. Making comparisons
5. Questioning
6. Identifying and fixing problems in understanding

READING GEOGRAPHY

Model 1

1. Connecting
2. Questioning, Picturing the text
3. Identifying and fixing problems in understanding
4. Making comments
5. Predicting what happens next

Model 2

1. Connecting
2. Identifying and fixing problems in understanding
3. Connecting
4. Identifying and fixing problems in understanding
5. Making comparisons
6. Picturing the text, Making comments
7. Questioning

Model 3

1. Making comparisons
2. Connecting
3. Making comments
4. Predicting what happens next
5. Questioning
6. Identifying and fixing problems in understanding
7. Picturing the text

Model 4

1. Predicting what happens next
2. Connecting
3. Identifying and fixing problems in understanding
4. Making comments
5. Questioning
6. Picturing the text
7. Making comments

Reading Social Studies

READING CIVICS

Model 1
1. Predicting what happens next
2. Connecting
3. Identifying and fixing problems in understanding
4. Making comments
5. Questioning
6. Making comments

Model 2
1. Making comments
2. Questioning
3. Picturing the text
4. Connecting
5. Predicting what happens next
6. Identifying and fixing problems in understanding

Model 3
1. Predicting what happens next
2. Questioning
3. Connecting
4. Identifying and fixing problems in understanding
5. Making comments
6. Making comparisons

Model 4
1. Predicting what happens next
2. Connecting
3. Identifying and fixing problems in understanding
4. Questioning
5. Picturing the text
6. Making comments